Parenting 101

A Mother and Teacher of 30 Years Shares Her Best Parenting Lessons to Raise Happy, Healthy, Responsible, and Successful Children From A to Z

HowExpert with Melanie Miller

Copyright HowExpert™
www.HowExpert.com

For more tips related to this topic, visit www.HowExpert.com/parenting.

Recommended Resources

- HowExpert.com – Quick 'How To' Guides on All Topics by Everyday Experts.
- HowExpert.com/books – HowExpert Books
- HowExpert.com/products – HowExpert Products
- HowExpert.com/courses – HowExpert Courses
- HowExpert.com/clothing – HowExpert Clothing
- HowExpert.com/membership – Learn All Topics from A to Z by Real Experts.
- HowExpert.com/affiliates – HowExpert Affiliate Program
- HowExpert.com/jobs – HowExpert Jobs
- HowExpert.com/writers – Write About Your #1 Passion/Knowledge/Expertise.
- YouTube.com/HowExpert – Subscribe to HowExpert YouTube.
- Instagram.com/HowExpert – Follow HowExpert on Instagram.
- Facebook.com/HowExpert – Follow HowExpert on Facebook.

COPYRIGHT, LEGAL NOTICE AND DISCLAIMER:

COPYRIGHT © BY HOWEXPERT™ (OWNED BY HOT METHODS). ALL RIGHTS RESERVED WORLDWIDE. NO PART OF THIS PUBLICATION MAY BE REPRODUCED IN ANY FORM OR BY ANY MEANS, INCLUDING SCANNING, PHOTOCOPYING, OR OTHERWISE WITHOUT PRIOR WRITTEN PERMISSION OF THE COPYRIGHT HOLDER.

DISCLAIMER AND TERMS OF USE: PLEASE NOTE THAT MUCH OF THIS PUBLICATION IS BASED ON PERSONAL EXPERIENCE AND ANECDOTAL EVIDENCE. ALTHOUGH THE AUTHOR AND PUBLISHER HAVE MADE EVERY REASONABLE ATTEMPT TO ACHIEVE COMPLETE ACCURACY OF THE CONTENT IN THIS GUIDE, THEY ASSUME NO RESPONSIBILITY FOR ERRORS OR OMISSIONS. ALSO, YOU SHOULD USE THIS INFORMATION AS YOU SEE FIT, AND AT YOUR OWN RISK. YOUR PARTICULAR SITUATION MAY NOT BE EXACTLY SUITED TO THE EXAMPLES ILLUSTRATED HERE; IN FACT, IT'S LIKELY THAT THEY WON'T BE THE SAME, AND YOU SHOULD ADJUST YOUR USE OF THE INFORMATION AND RECOMMENDATIONS ACCORDINGLY.

THE AUTHOR AND PUBLISHER DO NOT WARRANT THE PERFORMANCE, EFFECTIVENESS OR APPLICABILITY OF ANY SITES LISTED OR LINKED TO IN THIS BOOK. ALL LINKS ARE FOR INFORMATION PURPOSES ONLY AND ARE NOT WARRANTED FOR CONTENT, ACCURACY OR ANY OTHER IMPLIED OR EXPLICIT PURPOSE.

ANY TRADEMARKS, SERVICE MARKS, PRODUCT NAMES OR NAMED FEATURES ARE ASSUMED TO BE THE PROPERTY OF THEIR RESPECTIVE OWNERS, AND ARE USED ONLY FOR REFERENCE. THERE IS NO IMPLIED ENDORSEMENT IF WE USE ONE OF THESE TERMS.

NO PART OF THIS BOOK MAY BE REPRODUCED, STORED IN A RETRIEVAL SYSTEM, OR TRANSMITTED BY ANY OTHER MEANS: ELECTRONIC, MECHANICAL, PHOTOCOPYING, RECORDING, OR OTHERWISE, WITHOUT THE PRIOR WRITTEN PERMISSION OF THE AUTHOR.

ANY VIOLATION BY STEALING THIS BOOK OR DOWNLOADING OR SHARING IT ILLEGALLY WILL BE PROSECUTED BY LAWYERS TO THE FULLEST EXTENT. THIS PUBLICATION IS PROTECTED UNDER THE US COPYRIGHT ACT OF 1976 AND ALL OTHER APPLICABLE INTERNATIONAL, FEDERAL, STATE AND LOCAL LAWS AND ALL RIGHTS ARE RESERVED, INCLUDING RESALE RIGHTS: YOU ARE NOT ALLOWED TO GIVE OR SELL THIS GUIDE TO ANYONE ELSE.

THIS PUBLICATION IS DESIGNED TO PROVIDE ACCURATE AND AUTHORITATIVE INFORMATION WITH REGARD TO THE SUBJECT MATTER COVERED. IT IS SOLD WITH THE UNDERSTANDING THAT THE AUTHORS AND PUBLISHERS ARE NOT ENGAGED IN RENDERING LEGAL, FINANCIAL, OR OTHER PROFESSIONAL ADVICE. LAWS AND PRACTICES OFTEN VARY FROM STATE TO STATE AND IF LEGAL OR OTHER EXPERT ASSISTANCE IS REQUIRED, THE SERVICES OF A PROFESSIONAL SHOULD BE SOUGHT. THE AUTHORS AND PUBLISHER SPECIFICALLY DISCLAIM ANY LIABILITY THAT IS INCURRED FROM THE USE OR APPLICATION OF THE CONTENTS OF THIS BOOK.

COPYRIGHT BY HOWEXPERT™ (OWNED BY HOT METHODS)
ALL RIGHTS RESERVED WORLDWIDE.

Table of Contents

Recommended Resources 2
A Foreword from the Author 7
A 9
- *Accept the Challenge* 9
- *Acknowledge a Higher Power* 10
- *Admit Your Mistakes (Then Apologize)* 12
- *Allowance* 12

B 15
- *Babies* 15
- *Bless Your Children* 15
- *Bore Your Children to Death* 16
- *Build Them a Home, Not a House* 18

C 19
- *Channel a Strong Will Rather Than Break It* 19
- *Choose Your Battles* 20
- *Consistency is a Must* 22

D 24
- *Deserve the Respect You Expect* 24
- *Discipline* 25
- *Divorce* 26

E 29
- *Education Matters* 29
- *Encourage, Edify, and Empower Your Child* 34
- *Enjoy Your Kids* 35

F 37
- *Fair is for Carnival Rides and Cotton Candy* 37
- *Flexibility is Key* 38
- *Forgive, Forget, and Move Forward* 40

G 41
- *Get a Life (of Your Own)* 41
- *Get Off the Phone!* 42
- *Go With Your Gut* 43

H 46
- *Handle With Care* 46
- *Have Goals and Actively Work Towards Them* 47

I 49
- *Inspire* 49
- *It's Not Always About You* 50

J 52
- *Jobs* 52
- *Just Breathe* 54

K **57**
- *Keep on Keeping On* *57*
- *Keep the Channel Open by Keeping a Cool Head* *57*
- *Keep Your Eyes Open* *59*

L **60**
- *Less is More* *60*
- *Let Them Fail* *64*
- *Love Them*...*66*

M **69**
- *Make Them A Little Uncomfortable*......................................*69*
- *Meet Their Needs* *71*
- *Money* *73*
- *Moving Out*...*74*

N **77**
- *Never Say Never* *77*
- *Nip It In the Bud!* *77*
- *"No!" – Mean it When You Say It* *79*

O **82**
- *Obedience: Sometimes It's a Matter of Life and Death* *82*
- *Open House* *85*

P **87**
- *Parents, Not Friends* *87*
- *Playing One Parent Against Another* *89*
- *Punish With a Purpose*...*90*
- *Put Yourself in Their Shoes*..*92*

Q **94**
- *Quality versus Quantity*...*94*
- *Quiet* *95*
- *Quit* *97*

R **98**
- *Raise Them, Don't Grow Them* *98*
- *Read to Them* *98*
- *Role Models Matter* *100*

S **102**
- *Set Boundaries* *103*
- *Shaming* *104*
- *Shielding Your Children From Reality* *107*
- *Step-Parenting* *109*

T **112**
- *Take Advantage of Teachable Moments* *112*
- *Take Time (Because You Can't Make It)*..............................*113*
- *Talking to Your Kids About Sex* *114*
- *Transition With Your Children* *117*

Trophies	*118*
U	**122**
Unlearn Some Stuff	*122*
V	**124**
Validate Your Children	*124*
Value Your Children	*124*
Values	*125*
W	**127**
WalMart Rules	*127*
Whining	*128*
X	**130**
EXpectations	*130*
EXperiences	*130*
EXtreme Parenting	*131*
Y	**133**
You Get What You Get, and You Don't Throw a Fit!	*133*
You're the Boss	*133*
Youth is Temporary	*134*
Z	**135**
Zip Your Lip	*135*
Zits and Hormones	*136*
Zucchini Principal	*136*
About the Expert	**139**
Recommended Resources	**140**

A Foreword from the Author

Before you start reading this book I want you to know that I am serving up these offerings of advice with a great big heaping helping of humble pie. I wish I could say that the principles you see here are the result of the innate knowledge of a perfect parent who got it right the first time, but that would be a lie. The truth is, a lot of what you are about to read is the result of lessons learned from some colossal mistakes my husband and I made along the way as we were bringing up our children.

I am issuing this disclaimer for a couple of reasons. First of all, I am admitting that I made some huge blunders as a parent in order to give you hope. You will make a lot of mistakes as a parent, too. My children are living proof that these mistakes do not have to be fatal. Kids are kind of resilient and can absorb at least a few impacts before they suffer any permanent damage. The key is to pick up the pieces and patch them back together the *best* you can, as *fast* as you can. Then go forth and do better.

The second reason for this disclaimer is in case any of my kids ever get a hold of this book. I want to admit my screw-ups right up front and head off at the pass any accusations from them that I am the biggest hypocrite who ever lived. Believe me; if anybody knows my shortcomings as a parent, it's my three kids.

On a positive note, all three of my children have grown up to be successful, self-supporting adults. Although, I'm sure at least some of their success has occurred *despite* our parenting errors, I think my husband and I deserve *some* credit for producing productive citizens of society!

I am a high school teacher, and I could tell you some stories about what happens to kids who come from homes where the principles of this book are not practiced. It's not pretty. Of course, there are some exceptions. I have seen some kids who are better adjusted than they have a right to be. Some others came from pretty good homes and attentive parents and still turned out to be rotten eggs. All in all, though, if you implement best practices, you exponentially increase your odds of raising a decent person who won't embarrass you.

I hope you enjoy my book and that you are as blessed by reading it as I was by writing it!

Melanie Mathis Miller

2018

A

Accept the Challenge

Congratulations! Since you have selected this book to read, I assume you have already taken care of this first step by choosing to become a parent. Perhaps you are new to this parenting gig, and you want to read this book to get off on the right foot. Good for you! Maybe you are several years and multiple kids into this racket already, and you're reading this book to check up on yourself. If that's the case, then let me commend you for having an open mind and not being a know-it-all already. Or, maybe you're here because you have married someone with children and you are "stepping" into parenthood from that angle. If so, then bless your heart! I especially admire that you are reading a parenting book. It indicates that you take your new role seriously and not just by default of a matrimonial package deal; you actually want to get this *right*.

No matter what brought you here or what stage of parenting you are in, *welcome!* Make no doubt about it, parenting *is* a challenge. If you want to overcome and win at it, then keep reading. You will find some helpful tips and encouragement here to get you through this thing.

Acknowledge a Higher Power

This is not a faith-based book *per se,* but it *is* written from my own perspective, based upon my personal experiences and observations; therefore, since I am a Believer, I get to include this bit of "religiosity."

From the time my children were little, they have never left the house without hearing me or their father (or *both* of us) say to them, "Remember *Whose* you are," and because of their upbringing, they have always known exactly what that means. Notice the capitalization of the pronoun? That is not a mistake. That is how we reference Deity.

Parents often tell their children to remember *who* they are, and there is certainly nothing wrong with that. In fact, I encourage it. It is a reminder to them that they should carry themselves with dignity and never forget that they represent, not only themselves, but their family name and the others who wear it, as well.

The admonishment to remember *WHOSE* they are, though, takes the expectation to a higher plane. It raises the bar to enforce an even higher standard. It reminds them where they came from and where they are going and to act accordingly. When you are the child of a King, you know to behave like a prince or a princess.

Scripture tells us that we are "fearfully and wonderfully made." Even if you are not a believer in a higher power, I'm willing to bet you are at least somewhat impressed by the perfect symbiotic intricacies of the human body in its place in the universe. If so, then you may address the issue of acknowledging a higher power from that standpoint. Let your children be in awe of *something*. It instills healthy doses of both pride *and* humility – pride in the knowledge that our very existence illustrates the miraculous, and humility in the knowledge that man had absolutely nothing to do with making it happen. Every person needs this balance of self-awareness. Part of your job as a parent is to help your children to achieve that balance.

If you are indeed a Believer in God, though, then be aware of your responsibility to nurture your child's Spiritual needs. You already know you must meet their physical needs; even the law enforces *that*. Satisfying their innate hunger for their Creator, though, is something that you voluntarily choose to do. Do this, and your child can see that you, too, look to a higher authority. By demonstrating your own faith, you help them to develop theirs. If you have ever been through a really rough patch in your life, then you know how vital faith is. Help your children to grow their own. It is a gift that will sustain them for life.

Pray with your children. Read the Bible together, or whatever Holy Book you look to. Don't just *send* them to Sunday school, Church, Synagogue, or Mosque; go *with* them.

Admit Your Mistakes (Then Apologize)

This is just a good overall rule to live by. A willingness to say, "I was wrong; please forgive me" will go a long way towards mending the cracks in the seams of any relationship. It's rather hard to do, though. It can be especially hard to make yourself that vulnerable to a child. Do it anyway. Let your child know that you are human and that it is okay to be so. You may be surprised that they will actually admire you for it. Ironic, isn't it? It makes sense, though. Think of someone who has wronged you. Now think of how you would feel if that person never tried to make amends versus how you would feel if they approached you with sincere remorse. You don't mean to tell me that you prefer the former, do you? Of course not! So, if, by apologizing, a person stands *taller* in your estimation, tell me again how apologizing is a *humiliating* experience!

You want your children to own their mess-ups and make them right, don't you? Well, you are going to have to show them how that's done. If you can't do it, yourself, you can't very well expect *them* to.

Allowance

The question of paying children has long been debated. Ultimately, every household does what works for them.

No matter how you choose to handle the issue of allowances, though, this fact remains – Every child must, at some point, learn about money. He needs to learn the value of a dollar and how to manage money. He needs to learn the concept of delayed gratification by saving up for something he wants. He needs to learn that just because he says, "I want," things don't just magically appear; things must be paid for. The only way children can learn these lessons is to have some money of their own to practice with.

So how do you get that money into their hands without just forking it over for no apparent reason? If you don't teach them the concept that money is *earned,* then any other lessons regarding money seem kind of pointless.

Do you pay kids to do their chores? Here's my take on that. Every child needs to understand that he is a part of a family – a *team* – and every member has an integral role. Except for the baby, there are no freeloaders allowed. The chores a child does are what he contributes to that team. He needs to know that he is expected to perform these duties with or *without* pay. This is all part of teaching kids about responsibility and self-discipline.

I have no problem with telling a child that his payment for doing his chores is that he has a roof over his head, a bed to sleep in, food to eat, and clothes to wear. We have electricity, running water, television, and internet. Feel free to show him some of the bills versus your paycheck and let him see what a sweet deal he is getting financially.

If you want to get some money into his hands, perhaps, you can allow payment for jobs above and beyond their usual duties. Or just give him an age appropriate amount of cash each week to learn with. If he has been particularly unreliable about doing his chores that week, or has been an all around brat, then, by all means, don't give him a dime, and let him know why. You should probably give him a chance to earn it back, but that's up to you.

Your child will want to make some unwise purchases. He might save his money for months to buy something you know won't last a day. You can advise him, but resist the urge to stop him. This is also a valuable lesson that requires money to learn. The item he buys may not be worth it, but the lesson is.

B

Babies

My father has told me the story of how when I was born, he and my mother would try to care for me with me in one hand and a childcare book in the other. My grandmother noticed this one day and made the remark, "You know there's really not much to taking care of a baby; just keep one end fed and the other end dry."

When it comes to the basics of baby care, my grandma was pretty much right.

Bless Your Children

When my daughter got married, she wore white, and her father walked her down the aisle in true traditional fashion. But when it came time for the "giving away" of the bride, we did a bit of a switcheroo. Rather than asking, "Who gives this bride?" the minister asked us – and the entire audience – "Who gives their *blessing* to this union?" The many friends and family of both the bride *and* the groom joined us in declaring, "We do." Her brothers even threw in a couple of raucous whoops to show their approval!

Start blessing your children when they are young. When they tell you of their goals and dreams, resist the urge to be critical of their choices. Don't worry if your five year old declares that he aspires to be a circus clown someday. Chances are he will change his mind. But if you have shot down the circus clown idea, don't count on him filling you in on his change of plans later. In fact, depending upon your reaction, he may decide not to apprise you of what is happening in his life much at all!

Instead, respond to your child's declarations by helping him explore his areas of interest. Buy him books on the subject. Look into what kind of training he will need to reach that goal. Take him to meet some people who work in that field and let him ask questions. Don't push so hard, though, that he feels like he's letting you down when he says he has changed his mind and wants to pursue professional sandcastle building instead! Make him understand that whatever fork in the road he chooses, you are going that way, too. Let your child know he has your approval and support.

Approval is important. Your child wants to please you – until he discovers that he can't. Don't let that happen. Sometimes your child will do things that disappoint you; never let him feel that *he* is a disappointment, though.

Your child is a blessing. Return that blessing to him.

Bore Your Children to Death

Well, maybe not to *death*. The point is, boredom is not *necessarily* a bad thing. I credit my own mother for teaching me this lesson many years ago. I was probably about 8 years old when I made the mistake of telling my mother I was bored. Well, let me tell you, she found me plenty to do, right quick! I spent the rest of the afternoon folding laundry, dusting furniture, sweeping the floors, and a whole bunch of other stuff to fill my hours. I learned *never* to use the word "bored" in earshot of my mother ever again.

Another way my mother attacked child boredom was to buy me a bicycle and kick me out of the house until dinnertime. I'm afraid that in the world we live in today, that may no longer be safe in many communities. Too bad. It's our children's loss.

Experts will tell you that boredom often leads to creativity. Provide your children with plenty of basic art supplies. A ream of paper and a box of crayons is a good start. Heck, my kids got the benefit of an endless supply of my students' leftover worksheets to draw on the back of. Whatever works! Age appropriate scissors, glue sticks, and water colors are great, too. You might want to limit the glitter. Yeah, just go ahead and scratch glitter off the shopping list. Don't ask me how I know this.

Get them lots and lots of books. I regularly picked up the discards from the local library and shopped the used bookstores. Not only does plenty of reading material help your child to fill his open hours, but you may discover you have a budding writer in the family when your child decides to try his hand at a bit of writing, herself. See? Boredom leads to creativity.

But then again, you can always give them chores to do. That's productive, too. At least give them *something* to do. There's a lot of truth in the old saying, "Idle hands are the Devil's workshop." That's the ugly flipside to boredom. Let them experience it, but monitor it, too.

Build Them a *Home*, Not a *House*

A house is just brick and mortar, a little wood, a little concrete, and a little sheetrock. It *may* be filled with peace and joy and love, but not necessarily. A house is destructible. It can become infested with vermin, flood, catch fire, or be swept away by a good stiff wind.

Home is a safe place where you know you are loved and are always welcome. It *is* filled with peace and joy and love. A home is *in*destructible. The big bad wolf can huff and puff all he wants, but a home will stand. That's because a home is a place in the heart and not an address on a street. You carry it with you.

Which would you prefer to live in? Which one will you provide for your children?

C

Channel a Strong Will Rather Than Break It

I recently saw a meme on social media that said something along the lines of, "Someday I will be glad that my daughter is an independent, strong-willed individual who won't take 'No' for an answer . . . but not today, not in *this* grocery store!"

Whoever wrote that, I want to say, "I feel you!" This is some tricky territory for a parent. If you are the parent of this child, please resist the urge to beat him into submission, either physically *or* emotionally. That does not mean that you turn a blind eye and a deaf ear to tantrums and other bad behavior, though! Lay down the law when it comes to obedience and respect and whatever you have defined as acceptable behavior. More on that later. For now, let's talk about what to do with all that defiance and misdirected energy.

The strong-willed child often has a heightened sense of justice and fairness. That's why he bucks you. He perceives your expectations of him as being arbitrarily one-sided and he is trying in the only way he knows how to right the wrong and bring the parent-child relationship into balance. Unfortunately, he lacks the maturity to understand that you know what is best for him and that the parent-child relationship is not *supposed* to be balanced. So what are you to do with that?

Give your child something it's okay to say "No" *to*. If he wants what's fair, then show him true injustice and inequities in the world. Point out that some people do not have the advantages that he has and encourage him to become the kind of person who wants to make the world a better place. Take him to shelters for the underprivileged and let him volunteer alongside you. Impress upon him this is one way of saying "NO!" as you teach him to stand up against what is *really* wrong in the world instead of standing up against *you*.

If it's just a case of a kid wanting to be defiant, then teach him to say "NO" to bullies. Teach him to protect his person and be brave enough to say "NO" to inappropriate touching. Teach him your standards when it comes to vile or unhealthy habits and allow him to voice his "NO" to those things. Kids love the word "No." It's one of the first things they say, right after "dada." Give them opportunities to say it; just don't let them say it to *you*.

See? Don't break the child's will; just channel it in the right direction.

Choose Your Battles

My daughter had her own sense of style from an early age. She didn't mind wearing frilly dresses, just as long as she didn't have to wear shoes with them. If footwear was an absolute must, then she preferred her big brother's cast-off cowboy boots. As she grew older, she would experiment with some rather shocking hair colors. I could go on, but you get the idea.

Once, when she was about three, my parents were visiting for the weekend. My father noticed as we were leaving the house that his granddaughter had selected some mismatched attire to wear to church. He asked me if I was actually going to let her go out dressed like that. I shot him a glaring, "Don't even think about going there" look and prayed that she had not heard him.

To be fair to my dad, he lived in another state and was not around my children on a regular basis. He had never witnessed one of my daughter's meltdowns over being told to change clothes. I had already learned that as long as she was modestly covered and in attire appropriate for the weather, her clothing preference was *not* the hill I wanted to die on! Fighting that battle was a needless waste of energy that was just going to end in tears for both of us.

Save the warfare for things that matter. Put your foot down when she's heading into morally questionable territory. Say "Not on my watch!" when you catch her trying out some unhealthy habits or behaviors. But before going into battle mode, ask yourself if it is an issue that really *matters*. Be honest with your answer. If it's something superficial like clothes or hairstyle, let it go.

Let it go. Trust me on this one.

Consistency is a Must

Maintaining a consistent pattern of expectations and responses is one of parenting's toughest challenges. We get tired. I get it. Sometimes we don't have the energy to follow through, so a discipline matter which we met with swift repercussions yesterday might not even get a raised eyebrow from us today. Even though this is understandable, it is also stirring up a recipe for disaster.

Kids are gamblers. If they know there is a *chance* that they might get away with an infraction, they will take that chance. You might blow up, but, hey, then again, you might not. Win!

If you really don't want your kid to do that thing, then you have to demonstrate that it is important enough to you that you will address it *every* time they cross that line. The first time you let it slide, they *know* it must not really matter that much to you, and they will keep on doing it.

This is one reason that you must be very careful what you say "No" to. Don't use "No" unless you mean it, because it takes a lot of energy to back it up every time a kid challenges it.

A lack of consistency is also unfair. A child does not know where he stands with you if the rules are always changing. How would you like it if your boss berated you today for something he praised you for yesterday? Totally unfair, right? I generally couldn't care less if a kid throws a "That's not fair" up in my face, but if he's saying it as a result of your parental inconsistency, I'm sorry, but I'm siding with your kid on this one.

D

Deserve the Respect You Expect

Notice I did not say that you had to *earn* your child's respect. You are the parent; respect is the default. I never really got the whole concept of *earning* someone's respect anyway. I mean, what does that look like? Taken literally, it means that a person can treat you like something stuck to the bottom of their shoe until such time as you have proven yourself worthy of their esteem. Forget that!

Losing someone's respect, on the other hand, is an entirely different matter. Expect your child to show you and everyone else respect, but make sure you are a person of integrity and honor who deserves the recognition. And remember, once respect is lost, it is very difficult, if not impossible, to get back again.

Be the kind of person your child can look up to. Show them that you *deserve* their respect and, thereby, make it easy for them to give it to you.

While we are on the topic of respect, demonstrate it for them. Let them hear you say "Thank you" to the wait staff. Tack a "Please" onto your requests. Drive friendly. Basically, treat others the way you want to be treated. All the lecturing in the world will go in one ear and out the other, if you don't practice the principles, yourself. So, if you want to have respectful children, show them how.

Discipline

Let's make one thing clear right up front. *Discipline* is not the same thing as *punishment*. (We'll cover "punishment" under "P.") Discipline is what you instill in your child to help him to *avoid* punishment – and a whole lot of other negative consequences.

Discipline is about helping your child to adopt regular habits of exemplary behavior. In some homes, this means expecting the children to perform certain tasks each day such as making their beds, feeding the dog, carrying out the trash, completing their homework, etc. It also includes personal hygiene habits, such as bathing and brushing teeth. The jobs vary from household to household, depending upon what the parents deem to be appropriate and needed. The tasks need to be age and ability aligned, as well.

The initial goal is to establish the tasks as an expected routine to the point that the child quickly (or at least eventually!) comes to understand that he will be held accountable to perform them without being told or reminded. He will develop the *self-discipline* to make sure he gets the jobs done. At first, he may do them in order to avoid your ire or the incumbent punishment associated with failing to do them. After time, you will hopefully reach the ultimate goal of seeing your child do these things for the intrinsic reward they bring. You may have to facilitate this by informing them from time to time what those rewards are.

"See? Aren't you glad you brush your teeth every day? No nasty cavities for *you!*"

"Good thing you cleaned your room yesterday. Think how embarrassed you would have been if Aunt Martha had seen what it looked like *before* when she dropped in for a surprise visit today!"

"Look how glad Buster is to see you when you get off the school bus! He knows you are about to feed him!"

Helping your children to develop discipline to do the small things when they are young will translate into their becoming responsible adults who will have the discipline to have a work ethic, pay their bills, care for their families . . .

Divorce

I've not been divorced, myself, but I have seen enough of it that I have made some observations I can share.

In a word: co-parenting.

You may no longer be married to your child's other parent, but you do not get to leave your child rearing responsibilities behind with the other half of your assets. You have to share the kids, too. I'm not talking about paying your child support on time, either, although that is important. The courts will handle that. I'm talking about the day to day required interaction with your children such as discipline, hands on training, and just all-around participation in their lives. Divorce complicates it, but it doesn't negate it.

We'll start with the basics. Never badmouth your child's other parent in front of your child. Your child is half made up of their other parent's DNA and influence. When you denigrate your ex, you denigrate your child in his mind, even though your child isn't responsible for your' ex's choices.

From the other side, what if you are the parent who is being badmouthed. It hurts, but don't worry about it too much. Your kid isn't stupid. He probably knows it isn't true. It also helps to keep an open line of communication with your child so he feels comfortable *asking* you about some of the claims your ex makes. You can tell your side of the story, but don't go into the sordid details of what led to the divorce, either. Remember, don't paint your ex as the bad guy for your kid. Besides, if your ex truly is the spawn of Satan like you think he is, your child will figure it out eventually.

What if your ex takes on the role as the "fun" parent, leaving you with the day to day non-fun tasks of providing and disciplining? Again, your child will catch on to that, too. At the very latest, he'll figure it out when he has kids of his own and discovers that the fun part of parenting is the easy part, but the responsible part is kind of tough. In the end, your child will appreciate and respect the parent who was there for him and did the hard things.

When it comes to discipline, back the other parent's play. Refusing to do so puts your child in the middle of a dispute that is between you and your ex. I know a single mom who punished her teenage son for causing trouble at school by taking his truck away for a few weeks. He could ride the bus to school, but he needed to be picked up following his after-school practice later in the day. Because of the parents' conflicting work schedule, the dad had to go and get him. Dad didn't like that, at all. What dad needed to remember, though, is that he would have had to do that even if he and his child's mom were still together.

Don't mix parenting issues up with divorce issues. Your divorce and any incumbent hostilities between you and your ex is not your child's fault or problem.

E

Education Matters

Okay, I'm going to put on my teacher hat to talk you through this one.

Most kids have a tendency to rise to your level of expectation. At least they try to. That's because, despite their periods of being impudent brats, they do love you and want to please you. Set the bar high (but don't be unreasonable). Communicate that you expect them to achieve. Then stand back and be prepared to be impressed. Set the bar low and expect little, and that's exactly what you will get.

This principle applies in many areas, but particularly in education.

Here's one way of facilitating this objective: Be involved in your child's education. I'm not just talking about nagging him to do his homework. When your child is young, check his backpack every night, or at least a few times a week. You will find unfinished work in the bag of the kid who swears he has no homework. You will find some graded papers marked heavily in red ink in the bag of the child who answers "Fine" when you ask him how he's doing in school. Used to, you'd find notes from teacher, but in this age of email, that's probably a thing of the past. Your child's teacher probably has a website with a wealth of information you need to know. Check it out once in a while. Some scrutiny lets your kid know you are keeping an eye on his academic performance. That says that his education matters to you. And it should.

Attend open house at your child's school. If possible, volunteer. An occasional PTA meeting won't kill you, either. It's fine to contact your child's teacher when it is warranted, but please don't harass the poor woman.

When the teacher calls you and tells you that your little darling's behavior in the classroom has been less than exemplary, don't make excuses, and, for heaven's sake, don't turn and ask your child, "Is this true?" Of course, it's true! Do you seriously think a teacher wakes up in the morning and thinks to herself, "You know what? I think I'll make up a cockamamie story about one of my students today and tell his parents just so I can deal with the fallout! After all, I don't have anything better to do today!"

When you discuss this phone call with your child, and he says it's because his teacher doesn't like him, give this response the eye roll it deserves. I assure you, we teachers do not go into the profession so we can make kids' lives miserable. On the other hand, if it's true we don't like your kid, there's a darn good reason, and you can tell him so!

When your child is older, STILL attend open house and do the other stuff. I teach high school. On open house night at the elementary school campuses, the parking lot is full, cars are lined up down both sides of the street, and some park on the grass. Open house at the high school? Crickets. A few parents will drop in and ask in earnest how their children are doing. These are the parents of the straight A kids who read Chaucer and balance chemistry equations for fun. I do NOT need to see these parents. On the other hand, I believe there is a direct correlation between this parent's level of involvement and their child's success.

This kid knows he'd better toe the line, because if he doesn't, mom and dad will know of that situation immediately and they *will* do something about it. See what I mean about kids rising to expectations?

On the flipside. My weaker students have uninvolved parents. My very *worst* pupils have parents who are entirely unreachable. When I call the phone number listed in their child's file, I get that awful 3 tone beep and the message, "We're sorry. The number you are trying to reach is no longer in service." When I send an email, it will always come back marked "undeliverable." This kid will behave with impunity and make no academic progress whatsoever, because he knows I have no way to tell on him. It will catch up eventually, but kids don't understand eventualities. They live in the *now*.

Every parent wants to talk about homework. Here are a few pointers on this subject:

1. It's okay to coach your kids with their homework a bit, but don't do it for them. Yes, teacher knows when you write your kid's essay or you do their math. The composition does not match what your child produces in class. Nor does it quite follow the format we use in class. Also, you don't complete the math problems using the method your child has been told to use for this particular assignment. Just trust me when I tell you we know. We might not be able to prove it, but we *know*.
2. Does your child tell you night after night that he has no homework *ever?* He's lying.
3. When your child can't do his homework, don't be too quick to believe him when he says

teacher didn't explain it. That makes no sense. Of course, teacher explained it. We do not get a kick out of grading a bunch of homework assignments poorly done or only half completed. We delight in work well-done, and we explain it explicitly in hopes of getting to rejoice with our students in their success. A student's success is a measure of our own. If your child doesn't understand the assignment, there's a very good chance he was talking, texting, napping, doing *anything* but paying attention while teacher was teaching.

4. Does your child bring home tons of homework in every class each night, making you just seethe at how it cuts into your family time or their play time or extra-curricular activities, or mid-week church services, etc.? Do you find yourself judging the teachers for poor management of class time or for being insensitive to boundaries when it comes to assigning work that requires excessive time beyond school hours? Here's a secret most parents don't know. Most teachers give students class time to do their work. Again, your child is stuffing it into his backpack to do later and doing all kinds of other things in the classroom. Don't blame teacher. She has tried to redirect your kid, but, alas, we cannot put hands on him or make any real threats. *You* can, though. Make your child *wish* he had completed the work in class. Review the section of this book on the subject of *discipline*, if you must.

Are there exceptions to these scenarios? Of course there are. Some teachers are real jerks. You have them in every profession. But I deal with over 180 kids per day. 179 of them are doing exactly as I have described here. If you think your child is the one who is not, so does every other parent. Do the math.

Make your child understand that the responsibility for his education falls primarily on him. Don't let him blame someone else or other factors when he fails. Expect him to take ownership in his own education. After all, it is *his* education; he is the one who needs it and will be using it someday. If your child truly is struggling with his assignments, remember there is only so much a teacher can do for 35 kids in a 45 minute class period. Be reasonable in what you expect her to be able to accomplish. In this day and age of digitalization, there is no end of resources for help. Teach your child how to seek out the help he needs to learn what he must learn. No whining or cop outs allowed.

I used the word "struggling" above. I wish I had a dollar for every time a parent told me his kid is failing my class because he "struggles" with the subject. Actually, I'd like to pull out a dictionary and explain to him what the word "struggle" really means. It indicates a fight to overcome an obstacle. No, your child isn't struggling. He has merely run into an assignment or concept that he cannot just passively acquire. He has realized it is going to require some effort, and he has thrown in the towel because it isn't easy. He hasn't begun to struggle.

Okay, I have said a lot, and it probably seems as if I have strayed far from our purpose. I have my reasons, though. Follow through on what I have told you here, and it sends a message to your child. It tells him that in your book, *education matters*.

Encourage, Edify, and Empower Your Child

This is such an important charge, I feel like I should devote several pages to it. On the other hand, I feel as if the need to do these things is so obvious, I really shouldn't have to explain it at all!

It goes back to what we discussed previously. A child will rise to whatever level you set the bar for him. Don't set it high and then belittle and discourage him. Give him the tools to achieve. Be generous with the "Attaboys" and "Attagirls" when he experiences success along the way. Don't let him quit due to discouragement when he falls short of the goal. You get the idea.

And never underestimate the power you have over your child's ability to achieve.

It is harder than you think to bring someone up, but oh so easy to tear them down.

If you don't believe me, stand on a chair. Ask someone on the floor to hold your hand. Now try to pull them *up* onto the chair with you. Tough, isn't it?

Now, ask them to pull you *down* from the chair. See how easy that was? Probably didn't take much more than a gentle tug, did it?

Remember this little object lesson when dealing with your children. It's much easier to destroy a child than to lift him up. That is a scary amount of power to have over impressionable young minds. Don't abuse it.

Enjoy Your Kids

"Have kids," they said. "It'll be fun," they said.

Yeah, right! Raising kids is hard work. It's a 24/7 watch with no breaks, and it lasts for years.

Those years will go by a lot more smoothly and a lot faster, though, if you refuse to see your parenting job as nothing but unending drudgery. Kids *are* fun. They are funny, too. Kids say the darndest things. That's such a well-documented fact that a long time ago there was even a television program named that. Document the funny things your kids say. They will give you a chuckle someday when they are grown. They make great filler for wedding speeches, too.

Play with your kids. Run through the sprinkler with them. Take them to fun places. Laugh. Yes, you are the responsible adult, but you're still human and need some lighthearted levity in your life. Let your children be a source for some of that. After all, you brought them into the world. You might as well get some enjoyment out of them while you have them. You won't have them very long. Trust me. They grow up fast. That's not just a cliché.

Make some happy memories to look back on after they have moved on. You'll be glad you did, and so will they. Ask yourself, "How do I want my kids to remember their childhood when they are grown?" You are the one who will make that happen. Make it a happy memory and one that you are a part of.

F

Fair is for Carnival Rides and Cotton Candy

It's the dreaded phrase that every kid throws down as his ace in the hole when he doesn't get his way. He is certain it will be his winning hand: *"That's not fair!"*

He will probably draw that last one syllable word out into an elongated whine, letting it dance upon your last nerve. You will be tempted to fall for it just to make it stop. Don't.

The universally accepted understanding of "fair" means to give everyone equal amounts and access. Fair is not the goal when raising children. The goal is to give each child what he needs. This will vary from child to child.

When I was a kid, to keep me in line, my mother would tell me, "If you do ABC, then you will get XYZ." I would do anything to avoid the dreaded XYZ. Those were dire consequences.

My sister on the other hand, heard something entirely different. When mother issued to her the "If . . . then" statement, she lit up with excitement. "You mean I get a choice?" she seemed to say. You'd see only a split second of a wrinkled brow as she weighed the consequences XYZ against the pleasure she would get from doing ABC. "Totally worth it!" was her response, and she went on to do ABC to her heart's content.

Do you think our parents could raise the two of us by the same standards and methods and be equally successful in getting us safely to adulthood? Not a chance! You better believe there were some variations in how we were treated. Fair? Nope. Necessary? Yes, sir!

Are my sister and I comparably successful and equally responsible adults today? Pretty much. Sounds fair to me.

So what do you do when the one kid points out the inequities? You can tell him exactly why brother or sister gets something or some privilege he doesn't get and explain to him what he can do to *earn* the same. You are thereby giving him the *opportunity* to get the same as the sibling. Now, that's fair, don't you think?

Flexibility is Key

Flexibility is the capacity to return to one's original condition even after being extended and contorted. Lack of flexibility leads to one being "bent out of shape." No one wants to be bent out of shape. No one likes to be around somebody who is bent out of shape, either.

So, how does one avoid becoming this warped version of himself?

You start by understanding that rarely do things in life go exactly as planned. Moreover, you make up your mind to be okay with that. This principle applies to childrearing, too.

Throughout the months of pregnancy, your hopes and dreams for the unborn child grow and develop as he does in the womb. You know exactly how it's going to be. That little bundle of pink or blue will be perfect; he or she will be compliant and obedient, graduate at the top of the class, and will eventually become all the things you had hoped to be but have not quite attained, and so on.

Don't get too wrapped up in that fairy tale vision.

Be ready for a rough ride that will take you over some real bumpy places and crashing into unforeseen obstacles. You may even leave the tracks from time to time, but don't take leave of your senses when you do!

There will be illnesses, accidents, thwarted plans, dashed dreams, unplanned side trips – anything but the vision you created in the beginning. You have a choice. You can let these life realities destroy you, or you can just get over yourself, already. What right does any of us have to expect perfection, anyway? We don't. Accept the life you are given. Do what you can to avoid the pitfalls you can and minimize the damage to the best of your ability, but realize that there is no getting off the ride you're on until the train gets back to the station.

Hang on. It's going to get bumpy. There will be some really good parts, though. Enjoy them.

Forgive, Forget, and Move Forward

Everyone makes mistakes. Do you really need to be reminded of that fact? Even adults with plenty of life experiences behind them that should make them know better fall flat on their faces from time to time. It happens pretty often, actually.

How much more so is a *child* going to blow it? Kids haven't lived long enough to know better. Teach them. Understand that some of those lessons will come the hard way, rather than from a lecture from you. Think back on how you learned some of your own life lessons. Ouch! Some of them you'd rather forget. Your kids are no different.

When your children fail, by all means, let them experience the consequences, but forgive them and let them move on. Don't constantly remind them of the time they blew it, either. You know how you feel when someone does that to you. Why would you even want to inflict that nonsense on a kid?

That's the thing about that old maxim we call the Golden Rule – "Treat other people the way you want to be treated." It applies to everybody. It is perfectly viable to employ in how we treat children. That doesn't mean that kids are the same as adults. Common sense tells you better than that. It just means that they are human with human needs and feelings that should be considered the same as everyone else, even more so, because children are tender and impressionable.

G

Get a Life (of Your Own)

Kids take a lot of time and energy. You will invest hours and hours into them and their activities. This leads to your own life becoming inextricably entangled with theirs. That's okay but only up to a point. Once in a while you must extricate from them. Remember you are an individual. You had a life before you had kids, and, although some of your aspirations may have to be put on hold for a while, you haven't *died*. You are still there . . . *somewhere.*

There is nothing wrong with taking some time for yourself. It's only a problem if you are a narcissistic cretin who looks after his own needs at the expense of your innocent children. If you were that kind of person, I seriously doubt you would be reading this book, though.

Find a good babysitter and pay her well so she *wants* to be available when you need to take some time away from the kids. This is an investment with great returns.

So what do you do with these stolen moments? I don't know. What do you *want* to do? Take a class, read a book, write a book, exercise, visit a museum, go out for dinner, hang out with friends, ride a bike, take a hike, enjoy a hobby, learn a new hobby, join a club, go shopping, take a drive and stop and read all those historical roadside markers you pass everyday but have no idea what they say. Do *anything,* but get the heck away from those kids every once in a while.

They'll drive you out of your ever loving mind, if you don't!

Include your spouse in your plans. Sometimes this means that you take a break together. Your relationship must be maintained. If it weren't for your relationship, there wouldn't *be* any kids, but that doesn't mean that you *sacrifice* that relationship for them! After all, the kids are going to grow up and leave. If your relationship with their other parent has died in the intervening years, you will grow old all alone. Who wants that?!

Sometimes, including your spouse in your plans means taking over the child supervision duties so your other half gets his or her own much needed "me time." Golden Rule, remember? Play nice!

Get Off the Phone!

Do I really need to explain this one? The message here is *pay attention!* Kids get into a lot of mischief fast. When you are distracted, disasters happen. When you notice that the house is peaceful and quiet, be afraid, very afraid. Those little monsters are up to no good!

When my kids were about 8, 5, and 3, they came running into the house one day yelling at me to come see what they had found. I was on the phone, a landline, so I was bound by a cord to the kitchen wall. For 45 minutes, they intermittently ran outside to check on their "find" and then returned to tug at the hem of my shirt, and jump up and down, making pleading faces. I finally became so exasperated that I got off the phone and went outside to see what was so doggone urgent that they needed to be so rude.

They had a snapping turtle. A very *large* snapping turtle. It was so big, in fact, that it didn't even fit into the bed of their little red wagon (the largest kids wagon made, by the way). No, it rested on the sides of the wagon with several inches of its shell extending past both sides. No doubt, it took all three of them and possibly some help from the kid next door to lift it up there. Somebody could have lost a finger! Kids really do have guardian angels, I believe, but we shouldn't put them to unnecessary tests like I did that day!

Distractions also cause you to miss out on the important moments that you can't get back. Some of those moments may not seem important at the time, but they are rare chances for a *connection* with your child. Someday, you will realize how important those opportunities are and will regret the ones you missed.

Let someone else take the pictures. See the special moments of life with your own eyes and not through the lens of your cell phone camera. Don't let a stupid device *literally* come between you and your child.

Be *there*, in the *moment*, *with* her.

Go With Your Gut

Instinct is God-given. Don't be afraid to trust it and use it.

How many regretful parents have had to say, "I *thought* something wasn't right, but I couldn't quite put my finger on it?" They can put their finger on it, alright, once it's too late, though. How sad to recount all the signs you had that something was wrong *after* your child has done something so devastating that the damage is irreparable. There is no regret like the regret of hindsight when you have to admit that there was plenty of evidence beforehand that, had you been paying attention, you might have been able to avert the disaster and saved your child.

Does this sound dire? Melodramatic? Overplaying my hand? Maybe I am sensationalizing a bit, but not necessarily. We live in an age when kids take guns to school and kill their teachers and classmates. Children as young as 6 have been known to take their own lives over things that a mature adult would realize are just superficial life annoyances. Place yourself in the shoes of the parents of those children for a moment. Many of them will say, "I had no idea," but do you think if they *did* have an idea, they would tell us? I imagine they replay the days leading up to the terrible moment and recount all the signs that something was "off," that perhaps their child was trying to tell them something, that in some little way their child was crying for help.

Watch and listen for the signs. If something seems out of the ordinary, follow your instinct.

Has your child's behavior made you wonder if they are experimenting with drugs? There's a reason you are tuning into that feeling.

Do you wonder if something is happening at school that your child is reluctant to tell you about?

Is your son or daughter dating someone that gives off a vibe that makes you not quite trust him or her?

Unexplained in juries? Atypical moodiness? Furtive behavior? Keeping secrets?

Look into these things from the get-go. It's better to tick your kid off by being nosey now than to regret not doing so after it's too late.

H

Handle With Care

Kids are pretty resilient, but they are not unbreakable. They are sensitive and susceptible. Do not underestimate the impact you have on them.

Choose the words you say to them carefully. Whoever said that "Sticks and stones may break my bones, but words can never hurt me" was a fool. Careers, relationships, and lives have turned on the basis of mere words. Your words can either build your child up, or they can tear them down and kill their very soul within them.

I have said much so far about having expectations for your children to live up to. I mean that, but for heaven's sake, use some common sense! If your child is a fish, then don't judge him on his ability (or lack thereof) to climb a tree! Instead, give him a clean safe environment in which to swim and encourage him to be the best swimmer he can be.

Meet your child's physical, mental, emotional, and spiritual needs. They cannot satisfy them on their own. That's why God gave them parents. That's *your* job. I will speak more on the various needs children have a bit later, but I cannot possibly address everything you need to know about accomplishing all these objectives. I don't need to. Other people smarter than I am have already written those books. If you need to learn more about those things, then read some of those books and articles as soon as you finish this one.

It doesn't make sense to bring a child into the world just to destroy him or to allow him to wither. Take your job as a parent seriously *at all times*. You only have to drop a china plate once to break it. There are no second chances to fix some mistakes.

Have Goals and Actively Work Towards Them

Anything or anyone who is not making forward progress will grow stagnant and eventually die. Have you ever seen a stream of water that has been stopped from flowing? It gets this stinky scum on top. Don't be stinky scum.

Practice setting personal goals and progress towards their accomplishment. This is a dual blessing. You will enhance your own life, but you will also show your child how to enhance hers, as well.

Discuss your personal goals with your children and tell them what you are doing to make them happen. Then help your child to make some goals of her own. Make them age appropriate and attainable. Talk about the goal and help her to make and stick to a plan to see it to fruition. Cheer her on. Celebrate the milestones she reaches; encourage her when it gets hard or she has a setback.

When my oldest child was 5 years old, he announced that someday he was going to be a US Air Force pilot. We took him to a recruiting office and let him meet some fellows who could tell him a bit about that career. We showed him how to look up information on the Air Force Academy, because if you are going to aim, you might as well aim for the top. He also discovered the Merchant Marine Academy and read up on it, because it is a great way to enter the service as an officer, as well. He knew from the get-go the kinds of classes he would have to take in school and the grades he would have to make to realize his dream. Through a lot of hard work, and setbacks he had to overcome, my boy eventually landed a senatorial appointment to the Merchant Marine Academy at Kings Point, New York. The door to pilot training for the Air Force closed to him, but his goal was not thwarted. The Navy had a place for him, instead. Today, he is a Naval Flight Officer.

Do you think he would have made it that far if, when he told his father and me at the age of 5 that he wanted to fly in his nation's service, we had just said, "That's nice, dear?"

This habit of goal-setting will not only help your child to grow into a mature, well-rounded adult, but will also carry her through that adulthood as she continues to grow as an individual and becomes a better and better version of herself every day.

I

Inspire

Goal setting is a great thing, but not every child naturally picks up on the need to do so. Not only do you have to show them how by setting goals in your own life, but your child might need a bit of extra prodding.

Help your child to discover his interests, talents, and strong points, then gently suggest some goals which best fit his attributes. (By the way, resist the urge to pressure your child into following the dream that you wanted but never chased. Your child is not you.)

Read books to your child about the little engine that could and a whole bunch of other people who had a dream and lived it. When they are old enough to read on their own, make these kinds of books available to them. Tune them into appropriate videos and Ted Talks. Introduce them to people who are living their dreams. Let him hang posters on his bedroom walls that will remind him of his goals or encourage him to reach for them every single day. Encourage your child and let him know that you believe in him and his ability to fly.

It's Not Always About You

No one wants to be around a narcissistic, self-involved, self- promoting, egotistical know it all. Don't let your child become that guy.

How?

First of all, don't be like that, yourself. Duh.

Secondly, look for ways to teach your child empathy. Show him where and how people who are not so fortunate live. Get involved in charitable projects and take your children with you. Let them actively participate. Talk about these things. Talk about feelings. Look for teachable moments. If you and your child witness someone else's ill treatment, speculate together on how that person must feel and what would have been a better way to treat that person. Remind your child that what makes him feel bad, makes others feel bad, too. Encourage him to keep this in mind when he deals with other people.

In short, your child may be the center of *your* world – I know. You love him *that much* – but do not allow your child to grow up believing that the *whole* world revolves around him.

The world's a big colorful jigsaw puzzle made up of millions of pieces. He is just one piece. He is an important piece; the big world picture is not complete without him, but the same can be said for every other piece of the puzzle, as well. All together, we make a beautiful picture. All alone, not so much. Make sure your child understands this lesson. Work a jigsaw puzzle together with him and show him, if you must.

J

Jobs

What about when your child reaches the age that he can get a real job of his own, working part time after school and on weekends? That's fine. Some of the best lessons I learned in life came from these first jobs – how to manage my time and larger sums of money, how to deal with a difficult boss, how to talk to adults, and how to be responsible with larger duties than I had ever been given before.

Please keep a close eye on this, though. Your child's first and primary job at this point in life is to get an education. If the job interferes with that goal, then the job has to go. Make sure your child knows this starting out. It may give him an incentive to better manage his time to make both the job and school work out. Also, your child has the rest of his life to work. He is going to need that education to get the best shot at a job that will provide adequately for his needs. School comes first.

When a teenager gets a job, parents usually turn over a certain financial responsibility to the child. That's not a bad idea. Be reasonable, though. Every boy at the school where I teach wants a pick-up truck when he turns 16. You may steer him towards an older, used model that he can make the payments on. You may say he can have a truck if he can cover the insurance payments. (And we all know what automobile insurance for a teenaged boy runs!) Maybe you tell him he has to buy his own gas and pay for the maintenance on the vehicle. All of these are great ideas, but put all these expenses together, and your child will be headed towards a crisis. He's not an adult. He has to work up to the ability and wage earning capacity to take on that much.

Remember, your teenager may be taking on new and greater responsibilities by working a job, but she is not an adult yet. A couple of years ago, I had an 18 year old female student who kept falling asleep in class. It happened several days in a row, so I took her aside to try to find out what was going on. She told me she had been getting home from work at about 4:00 every morning. "What in the world kind of job are you working at that you don't get home until 4 am?!" I asked her.

She was bartending.

I didn't even know that 18 year olds were legally allowed to do that, but apparently they are. They just can't legally *drink* the beverages they serve. Anyway, the bar closed down at 2 am, then she had to help clean up before she could leave.

I understand that in some homes, money is tight, and even the children's income must be contributed to the family coffers. I get it. Economics are not equally distributed in society. But, for the love of all that's holy, do not let your 18 year old daughter schlep drinks for strange men in a bar and then drive herself home alone in the middle of the night. As a parent, please help your child find a safe and suitable way to play a financial role in the home. Sheesh!

Just Breathe

Remember what I said before about remaining flexible? Well, here is a piece of advice to help you do that.

Breathe.

No matter how bad it gets, life goes on. In the moment, you may wish the earth would open up and swallow you, ending it all, but that's not going to happen. Your train has not reached the station yet. Your heart will continue to beat, and it's going to need oxygenated blood.

Keep breathing.

My youngest child was a "kidder." He would make up crazy stories for the shock value – *my* shock – then laugh at my reaction. One day, he wasn't kidding, though. He was 14, and he and the other boys in the neighborhood were camping out at our neighborhood lake. They got the bright idea of going bike riding through the park about 10:30 at night. His front tire caught on the end of the sidewalk, catapulting him over the handle bars. He literally took a bite out of the concrete when he landed.

When he came into the house with his hand over his mouth to tell me he had busted out his front teeth (4 of them!), I rolled my eyes because I thought it was another one of his "jokes." When he pulled his hand away to show me the jagged edges where his teeth had once been, you can bet it took my breath away. I saw dollar signs in the blood around his mouth. I saw absences from school for him and from work for me as this was clearly going to result in multiple trips to the dental specialist covered by our insurance plan. His office is well over an hour away from our home. I realized all of this in an instant, and could hardly breathe.

My husband is better at taking things like this in stride. He took one look at the kid's mouth and said, "Yeah, that's gonna have to be fixed." That's it. He breathed right on through the crisis!

There will be sleepless nights, playground fights, and science fair projects you know nothing about until the night before they are due.

Breathe.

There will be broken bones, lost cell phones, and family vacations utterly ruined by a moody teenager.

Breathe.

You will have to explain to your little girl why her kitty didn't get to come home from the vet's office. You will hold her as her little heart breaks, and she sobs so hard that you have to remind her to . . .

Breathe.

Your son's team will make it to the tournament and advance to the final game which will be tied with one second left to go. Your son will have the ball at this crucial moment. He will shoot . . . and he will miss. You will have to walk next to him as you make your way through the parking lot to your car. Put your finger under his chin and gently lift. Make him hold his head up . . .

And breathe.

There will be premature babies who cling to life in the NICU for weeks. You may not get to bring yours home. *I am so sorry.*

Take a deep breath. Just breathe.

K

Keep on Keeping On

This is what you do after you master the technique of "Just Breathe."

Breathing in the face of adversity is merely the acknowledgement that life goes on no matter what disaster strikes. Keeping on is the act of putting one foot in front of the other and doing what comes next. It is deciding what must be done and doing it, whether it be damage control or stepping away from the chaos and starting over.

This is an important part of raising children. One, because no matter what calamity happens, as long as your child survives it, his life doesn't end there. You must finish raising that child. Two, you keep on keeping on, because your child needs to see you doing this. You must exemplify fortitude and courage. Show your child what that looks like in action.

Don't be a quitter. Don't raise a quitter, either.

Keep the Channel Open by Keeping a Cool Head

No matter what your child confides in you, do not freak out. Okay, you might be freaking out, but keep the emotional turmoil so well hidden that your child doesn't even suspect that you are about to lose it.

Whatever it is he tells you, act like it is perfectly natural for him to let you know. Act like you half expected him to bring it to you, even. Yes, I know it is all an act, but be glad and relieved that he trusts you enough to bring this bit of news to you. Consider the alternative. What if he had not told you? Or what if he went to the wrong person to seek help from and ended up in even deeper trouble?

If you act shocked, angry, or overly judgmental, you can bet he will never tell you anything again. That is a situation you want to avoid at all cost.

If he reveals that he is participating in a dangerous, illegal, or unhealthy activity, do not allow your default to be to determine how he must be punished. He may need punishment, alright, but first he needs help. That's why he came to you. The revelation he has made is his cry for that help. You are the parent, and it is your responsibility to get it for him.

The help he needs is entirely dependent upon what it is he is battling.

Are the people he is hanging out with a bad influence? He is asking, *begging,* you to forbid him from seeing them again. He isn't strong enough to resist their peer pressure on his own, and he realizes that. He needs you to play the part of the "heavy" so he can blame his separation from these kids on you. Be happy to fill this role. There is nothing wrong with being the bad guy, if it protects your child.

He might need medical intervention, or legal advice, or financial assistance. He might just need you to listen and to offer some sound advice.

Not all communication between parents and children is bedtime stories and chit chat at the dinner table. Sometimes, it can get deep and even appalling. Whatever it is your child needs to tell you, keep the channel wide open for that communication, though. You don't want to miss that call.

Keep Your Eyes Open

I think we have adequately covered this subject under the topics of "Get Off the Phone" and "Go With Your Gut." It's all about paying attention to what your child is saying and doing. Don't let anything get past you. Just wanted to give you one more reminder before we move on to the "L's."

L

Less is More

Don't let your kids have everything they want. They will ask for the sun, moon, and stars. It's only natural. The way they see it, it can't hurt to ask, right? If you don't ask, you won't receive. Plus, in the asking, they are informing you what it is they want. You need to know that bit of information for when you *do* intend to buy them something, after all. And if they know they are only going to get a percentage of what they ask for, then the more they ask for, the more they will get. They're young, but they're not stupid, you know!

When my kids were little, they had quite lengthy wish lists for Christmas. They learned pretty early on that they would get something from the list but not everything. Their father and I knew what it was they most wanted, and we tried to get that and some smaller things, as well. Christmas is a lot of fun, but if you have to go into debt to make it happen, you've missed the point of the holiday, and, worse, created the wrong image of Christmas (and life) in the hearts and minds of your children.

Kids love the lead-up to the holiday season. It is very easy for them to get caught up in the anticipation of what they will find under the tree for them. Without getting preachy, steer your kids away from the "getting" aspect of Christmas. Nourish a spirit of giving, instead.

There are plenty of charitable activities during the holiday season, Get involved and include your children. (But remember, the needs that are met by these charitable opportunities continue throughout the year and not just from Thanksgiving to Christmas!)

Involve your children in holiday baking. Give them age appropriate tasks in the kitchen, and make it fun. Let them decorate cookies. Deliver some to the neighbors.

Include children in the decorating process. Let them make decorations, as well. Focus on making it fun and not perfect. One year when my kids were very small, I was taking classes at the university. I had a choice between decorating for Christmas or studying for final exams, it seemed, so I delegated the job of decorating the Christmas tree to the kids. The bottom third of the tree looked great. The upper 2/3 which they couldn't reach was kind of bare. It was beautiful. That tree reflected where our family was at that point in time, and my children were thrilled that they got to help. They were so proud! The tree may have looked a little *less than* that year, but there was so much *more* to be enjoyed from the experience.

When my children were young, we started the tradition of Christmas caroling in our neighborhood. The first time we did it, it happened kind of by accident. School was out for the winter break and the neighborhood kids were at my house, as usual. They were getting bored and restless. I had a stack of frozen pizzas in the freezer that I had bought on sale. I also had several packets of Kool-Aid. I decided to turn it into a party. All the kids called their parents to ask if they could stay at my house a bit longer. Of course, the other moms were quite happy to have their kids out of their hair for a couple more hours. We had a quick practice session then went around the neighborhood, singing Christmas songs door to door. After that, we went back to our house for pizza and Kool-Aid. It was cheap, but it was fun. It was the perfect example of how less is more, and it became an annual tradition until the kids were old enough they didn't think it was so cool, anymore.

The point is to curb the childish tendency to think that Christmas is all about how many presents they get before they ever develop that perception. There is more to Christmas than that. Less is more, when it comes to presents.

Our family never got too carried away with birthday celebrations, but I don't personally have anything against birthday parties for kids. The only thing that puzzles me about them is how it appears to have become a competition these days. Parents want their child to have a bigger and better party than their friends have had. Then the parents of the next birthday child have got to up the ante and surpass the previous party. I've seen weddings that didn't cost as much as a five year old's birthday party! They rent entire restaurants or halls, hire entertainers, and set up an attended petting zoo. Every kid gets a bag of cheap gifts so nobody feels left out during the gift-giving. I wouldn't be a bit surprised if toddlers have gift registries.

Here's the deal. Kids. Don't. Care. This is all about the *parents* and how they feel they must put on a show to prove something. Maybe they are trying to project an image to impress the other parents. Maybe they feel inadequate as parents and are trying to prove their love for their kids. Whatever it is, they need to stop. A homemade cake or one from the grocery store and a few games in the backyard will do just fine. I promise. Less is more.

Even your lifestyle can reflect the "less is more" philosophy. Our house is kind of old, and it is mostly decorated with dollar store finds. Our community has a couple of high end neighborhoods, and all the kids go to the same school. Inevitably, that meant that my children had some friends from the other end of the socio-economic scale. I used to wonder if they compared our home with the homes of their friends. I know they must have. But you know what? Guess whose house the kids always wanted to hang out at? Yep. You guessed it. *Ours.* Those rich kids would even comment how much fun they had at my house. They weren't scared to death of what might happen if they accidently broke something. I didn't follow them around like a nervous wreck moving valuable items out of harm's way.

I was the cool mom, and all it required was having a house and habits that reflected that our family lived well within our means.

"Less is more" is totally worth it when you have kids. Teaching your children to find joy and contentment in having little and to be able to know the difference between "wants" and "needs" are valuable lessons that will carry them all the way through life.

Let Them Fail

It is a natural tendency to protect our children. When they are taking their first steps, we hover over them to catch them when they inevitably fall. There comes a point, though, when parents have to step aside and let them take a dive. It's probably more painful for us than it is for the child, to tell you the truth. So when you step in and try to keep your child from suffering the consequences of his failures or bad choices, who are you really trying to protect – your child or yourself?

Let's face it, we do suffer when our kid fails. You might be the parent who thinks your kid's behavior is a reflection on you, so you want your child to avoid failure so they don't make *you* look bad. Or maybe you don't want your kid to fail, because failure often leads to a mess that has to be cleaned up. Maybe you really do think you are doing what is best for your child when you intervene on his behalf when he fails.

Whatever your motivation, you are doing your child no favors. There are valuable life lessons to be learned in failure. Often, the payment for failure is the natural consequence of a choice. You are getting exactly what you deserve. Normal people feel a sense of wanting to see justice done when someone messes up. They don't necessarily feel that way when the person who messes up is their child. That's a shame.

When your child fails, he learns not to do that again. If he is not allowed to suffer the consequences, he doesn't learn that lesson. In fact, the absence of consequences will *reinforce* the bad behavior. Might as well do it again, if nothing bad is going to happen as a result, right?

As a teacher, I deal with several parents a month who contact me to intervene on behalf of their teenaged children in an attempt to waive off the consequences of their kids' choices.

"What can Brittany do to bring up her grade?" (Why are *you* asking instead of Brittany?)

"Can Damien have extra credit?" (Damien hasn't done the *required* work; how would more count as *extra?)*

"Savannah had a softball game that went late last night; can she have extra time to do her assignment?" (Never mind that it was assigned three weeks ago, and Savannah had class time to do the work, but played with her phone every day, instead.)

"My child has an IEP and gets accommodations. You had better be able to document that you have provided every one of those. I *will* be contacting my lawyer!" (I did the accommodations; did your child do *her* part?)

"Justin is failing your class and may not graduate!" (And?????) I'm curious. Why are Justin's parents more worried about the situation than Justin is? Here's your answer: Justin is accustomed to having his parents swoop in to save him from his laziness and bad choices. He's not worried, because he figures they will get him out of this mess just like they have all the others. Let. Him. Fail. Just once. He can go to summer school. He's 18. Don't you think it's about time to let him learn this fact of life?

Are you protecting your children from the consequences of their choices? You are robbing them of the experiences which will make them grow into mature and responsible adults. Stop it. Stop it. STOP IT!

Love Them

This one seems like a no-brainer. If you were the kind of parent who needed to be told this, you wouldn't be reading this right now. So, I'll just make some observations on the subject and leave it at that.

A popular expression I have seen around a lot lately is to "love *on*" someone. I've seen it on marquee signs in front of churches – "Come visit us for worship and let us love on you!" I've heard it in teacher inservices – "Make a difference in the lives of your students by loving on them!"

Huh? The phraseology alone belies the superficiality of the statement. Love *on*? You mean you apply love like a cheap hand cream or topical ointment? Do you really want love only to hit the surface without ever getting down deep all the way to the heart? If that's the level of love you think kids need, then please visit your doctor and find out what type of birth control is best for you.

To love *on* is not love at all. It is a fake show. It may look like love, but when tested – and kids *do* test us -- the recipient finds out real quickly how insincere that so-called love is. Kids may be dumb about a lot of things, but one thing is for sure – they can spot a phony a mile away.

If you have children, you will have to supply them with an abundant and never-ending supply of *real* love. It's the unconditional kind of love that is a sure thing through any and every circumstance. I have known parents who grow cold and distant when their child messes up. I believe these parents love their children, but they mistakenly believe this is an appropriate method of punishment or discipline. *It is not.*

Children – and most adults, as well – see the withholding of affection as the absence of love, and with good reason. This reaction to a child's mistakes screams, "I only love you when you please me." Children spend a lot of time displeasing their parents. They can't help it. They are still growing and learning. They don't know better yet. Please tell me that you don't turn off your love for them as they progress through this natural process of growing up, this series of mistakes and learning from those mistakes. That's just sick.

Sometimes – okay, a lot of times – kids do need some punitive results for their behavior. Please choose more appropriate means than withholding affection/love. Make sure your kids know that you love them even when they let you down, even when you are disappointed or angry with them. We will cover this part of the equation more in depth when we get to "P for Punishment" later on.

M

Make Them A Little Uncomfortable

At the time of this writing, a major news story has been about a 30 year old man whose parents had to take to court to get him out of their house. Apparently, a failure to launch is a real thing and not merely the premise of a light-hearted movie starring Matthew McConaughey. I am not going to pretend I know all the circumstances surrounding this court case or expound on who is or isn't at fault. I am going to give you a bit of advice for how you might avoid this situation in your own home, though.

A lot of parenting practices require a balancing act. You want to be firm but fair, loving but not permissive, fun but not irresponsible, protective but not smothering, and so on. Another balance which parents must achieve is in the atmosphere they create within the home.

On the one hand, you want to provide for your child's needs and even beyond by providing some of their "wants," as well. You put a safe roof over their heads. You make sure your children never go hungry, even if it means you miss a meal or two, yourself. You clothe them. They may not wear haute couture, but they certainly aren't naked. When they are sick, you take them to the doctor and pay for whatever medications they require. You take them on family vacations and run up an unholy Visa bill at Disney World. You get the idea.

Here's the problem. What kid is going to want to leave that padded nest? That's where the balancing act comes in. You have to make them *want* to leave. That doesn't mean that you create an intolerable atmosphere they feel they must escape, though. So, how does a parent achieve that? How do you provide them with a comfortable home but make them willingly walk away from it when the time comes?

Make them just a little uncomfortable.

Remember how we have discussed setting a high bar and placing expectations upon our children? Keep that up. Someday you will hear, if you have not heard already, your child explode and yell, "I can't wait until I grow up and move out where I don't have any rules!" He may punctuate the exclamation by slamming his bedroom door – the door to the bedroom in *your* house which *you* pay for.

You could give your child a lesson in irony at this point, or lecture him about how adulthood comes with more rules, not fewer, but it isn't really necessary. He'll figure it out someday when he is grown and has kids of his own. Just smile and calmly sip your coffee as you look forward to his eventual come-uppance. Smile because you have done your job. Although you may not be pleased with your child's angry outburst, it is actually a desired goal. You *want* your child to want to move out.

A child who moves out – and is able to *stay* out – on his own is evidence of the completion of a parent's job. Your role is to nurture, provide for, and train your child to become an independent adult who can function as a responsible and contributing citizen of the world. With perhaps a few exceptions, the man-child who never reaches that point is more a reflection on his parents than on himself.

Meet Their Needs

Children – humans, really – have so many more needs than just physical ones. It goes without saying that you must provide for your child's physical safety and well-being. If you neglect to do so, you could find yourself in a lot of trouble and even have your children removed from your home. If you want to be a good parent, though, you want to meet their other needs, as well.

They have emotional needs. As we have discussed before, they need to know without any doubt that they are loved and valued. Don't just tell your children you love them. Tell them they exist because you *wanted* them and *still* want them. Tell them how much happier you are now that they are a part of your life. Convey that they have intrinsic value just for being who they are.

They have mental needs. Nurture their minds as well as their bodies. Make school a priority, but don't relegate all of their education to hired teachers. You are your child's first and foremost teacher. Look for teachable moments and take advantage of them. Provide them with intellectual opportunities by taking them to museums, going on nature hikes and showing them the flora and fauna, reading to them, providing them with ample reading material, and so on.

When I was a child, my father inadvertently met some of my mental needs one day. A travelling book salesman came to our home selling World Book Encyclopedias and Dictionaries. Obviously, this was quite a few years ago. I know those books were expensive, but they were beyond value in helping me complete a lot of homework assignments, and when I was curious about something, 9 times out of 10, I could find out about it in one of those lovely hard-bound volumes. Sometimes, I just got bored, and – wait for it – I actually *read* encyclopedias. A huge percentage of the knowledge I have today came from rainy afternoons curled up on the couch with one of those books.

Today, that kind of knowledge is stored online, so instead of a set of encyclopedias, you will need to provide reliable internet service. That's great! Just monitor its usage, okay? There is a lot out there in the digital world that will destroy your child's mind as well as build it, and you want to guard against that.

They have *spiritual* needs. Every living thing has a need to want to know from whence it comes. There is something planted in the heart that makes it want to acknowledge, know, and worship that higher power and source of origin. Regardless of your own feelings on religious affairs, if and when your child shows a longing to embrace spiritual matters, do not squelch that. His curiosity is evidence that this is a need he has. Allow for that. If your family does practice a particular faith, then, of course, you will bring your child up in it. Your faith satisfies a need within you, so you will want to pass that on to your own child. It is a type of legacy.

Money

We have already covered allowances and jobs, so I won't rehash that here. I do have a little more to say about money issues, though, so I will do that.

Don't make financial issues your child's problem. If money is short, that is your job to take care of, not your child's. Can you discuss household financial matters in front of your kids? Sure, but limit this kind of talk, okay? If your children perceive that you are worried or scared, how do you think that makes them feel? You are their secure shield against the world. If your child sees you doubtful of your ability to fulfill that role, that could terrify him! Imagine yourself boarding a plane and seeing the pilot wringing his hands and worrying aloud about not having enough fuel to reach the destination. Now imagine that you are completely at the mercy of the airline and are not allowed to get off the plane before take-off. Yeah. It's like that.

You also want to keep financial talk within check, because there isn't a thing your child can do about it, anyway. My own dad used to call "family meetings" where he would set us kids down and lecture about how he had to go into savings just to pay that month's bills. He'd pace back and forth and swing his arms up and down for emphasis. Clearly, he meant to impress something upon us, but we weren't really sure what. I mean, we could do little things like turn the lights out when we left a room and try not to be wasteful, but we were already trying to be mindful of those things. We knew not to ask for too many things or privileges that required money. What could we do beyond that? We had no control over what stuff cost. Nor did we really understand what he was talking about. We were just kids. When he made that comment about dipping into savings to pay the bills, all I thought was, "Well, thank God we have savings, or we'd be in trouble!"

Here's my point. Teach your children not to be wasteful. Show them how to shop wisely by discussing how you make purchasing decisions by considering cost and quality. Inform them they cannot have everything they want. Make them understand Dad is not an ATM. Let them manage a little money of their own. Talk about the family's finances a little, but don't scare them or make them feel guilty for shortfalls in the family budget. Those aren't their fault or their responsibility.

Moving Out

Most kids need a transition period from your home to living on their own. This varies from person to person and household to household, but, traditionally, this transition period has been college. The college years were my own children's time of transition.

This was not something we just sprang on them at high school graduation, by the way. We began by discussing it with them when they were still in elementary school. My husband made a deal with them. If they made good grades in school and could gain acceptance to a four year university upon completing high school, we would allow them to go directly from high school to university rather than live at home to complete their first two years of school at the local community college.

This was expensive for us. Allowing your kids to live at home and go to community college before transferring to a university saves literally *thousands* of dollars. Plus, not every high school graduate is mature enough for that transition. It worked out for our family, though. First, it was an incentive for them to do well in school as they were growing up. Secondly, they saw moving out as a reward.

Now, they weren't immediately independent upon moving away to the university, by any means. We were still paying their way, and they knew they had to behave themselves and make the grades, or we would move them back home to community college in a New York minute. That's why it's called a transition. The point is, it put enough distance between them and their childhood home and gave them just enough taste of freedom that they knew they wanted to stay gone. They did behave well in school and they did make the required grades. We worked our rear ends off to keep our end of the bargain to pay for it. As a result, every one of them graduated with jobs in their fields, and they never moved back home except for summer breaks. Unlike their friends, they graduated debt free and did not have to live at home to be able to repay student loans, either. Expensive? You bet. Worth it? Absolutely! It was an investment we have never regretted.

This story is about how we did it for our kids. It may not be a feasible method for you. Economic realities vary from home to home, and I get that. There are other ways.

I have heard of several parents who charge their kids "rent" when they are old enough to have a job. It's usually a token amount, but it's enough to teach them how the grown-up world works. What the kids don't know, however, is that their parents are not actually using that money for household expenses. They are setting it aside in a separate bank account to return to their children to pay for moving out expenses such as that expensive first and last months' rent, security and utility deposits, furniture, and necessary household items. Moving out is expensive, and the young person who has enough to pay his own way may still not have quite enough for these start-up costs. These parents have foresight as they are able to return the rent funds to their children to cover these expenses. Moreover, the kids know that they actually earned that money themselves, so there is a bit of self-satisfaction in that.

Many years ago, teenaged girls were given what was called a "hope chest," usually for their 16th birthday. They would purchase, little by little, various household items they would need someday for their future home and store it in this cedar box for safekeeping until that day. I'm not sure why that practice ever ended, but maybe it's a good idea to bring it back.

You will have to come up with a plan for how you will help your child make his shift from your home to his own. Whatever plan you choose to implement, I hope it works out. You'll be glad when it does, and so will your kids.

N

Never Say Never

When you see somebody else's kid being a little twerp, do not say, "My child will/would *never* do that!" God has a sense of humor and He *will* make you the butt of His colossal joke.

How I wish I had a video camera in my classroom so I could show film clips to my students' parents who respond to my calls home with that statement, too. Yes, your child will do the things you think he won't. There's a good chance he's already doing them. Take off the rose-colored glasses.

Nip It In the Bud!

If you're old enough or watch reruns of old television shows, you are probably familiar with Deputy Barney Fife of *The Andy Griffith Show*. Whenever ole Barney got wind of any shenanigans going on in the town of Mayberry, he'd tell Sheriff Taylor it was time to "Nip that in the bud" before they had a full blown crime spree on their hands. It's good parenting advice, too.

Do you detect a "tone" in your daughter's voice when she responds to your direction? Firmly call her attention to it the first time it happens. Let her know that it isn't going to slip by unnoticed or unaddressed, and make it clear it will not happen again without consequences. Nip that little display of attitude in the bud before it grows into full rebellion, because that is exactly what it will do. Every time you allow her to get away with disrespect, she will be emboldened to do it again with increased intensity each time. Nope. Ain't gonna happen. Not on my watch.

Is your son growing lax about completing his homework or his household chores. Don't wait until this tendency towards laziness or neglect has evolved into a regular habit that is hard to break. If teacher calls home and tells you he has missing assignments, make him do them right then and there before he gets to enjoy any fun or free time activities. If teacher says she will not accept those late assignments for credit? Even better. Make him do them anyway. That'll teach him. Chores not done? Stand over him until they are. Add an extra one or two to make your point. Nip it in the bud. Be consistent about this, and he'll get back on track. (Go back and reread the section on "Consistency" to review how vital this component of the equation is, if you need to.)

Has your child told a white lie? Don't wait until he has told a big ole whopper that creates a huge mess before you nip that act in the bud.

Did she steal a piece of penny candy in the check-out aisle at the grocery store? Make her confess, pay, and apologize. What? Are you going to wait until you have to bail her out and pick her up at the police station someday? You may scoff and say I am overplaying it, but you know the felon car thief started *somewhere*. This is one lesson you don't want to learn the hard way. Nip it in the bud long before it gets that far.

Teach your children the concept of *integrity* – the practice of doing the right thing, even when no one is looking. You see, that's why kids try out these small infractions. They figure they can get away with them, because people tend to overlook small things. No one is *looking* for them. Since kids can get away with those things, they keep doing them and escalating them. Let your kids know you are, indeed, looking. In fact you are keeping a close eye out at all times, because you are prepared to *nip that activity in the bud!*

"No!" – Mean it When You Say It

Be careful what you say "No" to, because you are going to have to back it up. Some kids will make you have to back it up for a loooooooong time. They keep asking, begging, nagging, complaining, and trying to bargain with you to get you to back down. The minute you cave in, the kid has not only won, but you have created a monster and unleashed him. He will go on to terrorize you and everyone else he meets who tells him he cannot have his way.

It's common sense, really. When this kid figures out that his whiney wheedling methods will eventually work, he will use them. It doesn't matter that you have the ability to hold out against this kid for *days* before you succumb. He'll wait . . . as long as he knows he will get what he wants in the end.

As a teacher, I can spot these kids early on in the school year. The first time they ask for something and I tell them "No," they start in immediately.

"But why?"

"That's not fair!"

"You let *her*."

"My other teachers let me."

"You just don't like me."

"Oh my GAWSH! You are so *mean*!"

"I hate you!"

Ad nauseum.

The kid can't just accept my "No" for an answer and let it drop. He has been conditioned by spineless parents to believe that if he pushes hard enough, long enough, he will eventually get his way. Then when he comes up against a hard-nosed, no-nonsense teacher who digs in her heels and pushes back, he absolutely loses it. He can't handle it, because he has never encountered anybody who told him "No" and stood their ground.

You should see some of the angry explosions I have witnessed. The worst part is all the time that gets wasted as this kid disrupts my entire class to go through his process of trying to break me down. He robs every single kid in the class of valuable education time. I could cave in, but then I will have created a classroom climate in which I will never be able to deny a student anything. The kids will be completely in control of the class, which means there will be no control, at all. You cannot teach anything in a classroom like that.

Parents, this is *your* fault.

Do you have any idea how many of these kids I have later read about in the local paper for bowing up against law enforcement or resisting arrest? That is exactly where that kind of conditioning leads to.

Ironically, one key of managing this train wreck waiting to happen is *not* to say "No" more often. You need to think a bit before saying "No" and ask yourself a few questions first. Is this something that I feel so strongly about that I absolutely must deny it? Would saying "Yes" really be that bad? Is it really that important? Will it matter in the long run? Do I have the fortitude to hold firm to my "No" when he decides to challenge it? These are all things you will have to consider every time you tell your kid "No."

If after giving it careful consideration, you decide that the answer must indeed be "No," then stick to it. Under no circumstances can you back down. Even if you reconsider later and decide that your "No" may have been hasty, think long and hard about recalling it, because the consequences of doing so are *that* bad.

O

Obedience: Sometimes It's a Matter of Life and Death

Why do responsible dog owners put their dogs through obedience training? One reason is so their dog knows how to behave and interact politely. Another reason is for the dog's own safety. A dog that won't come when you call him is likely to run out into traffic and get run over.

Children need to learn to obey for much the same reasons.

I have known a few self-defined "liberal" parents who believe it is wrong to expect their children to obey blindly and without question. They prefer more "balance" in the parent-child relationship and do not want to create a situation where the parent appears to be a domineering bully which the child must succumb to in fear. They are certain the child raised this way will grow up to have all kinds of "issues."

God, help us!

I also know some other parents who lean that direction, but cushion their stance a bit by *explaining* to their children their reasons for everything they tell (ask?) them to do. I guess it *can* be okay to explain to your child why he can and cannot do certain things. I vividly remember the day my mother told me I was not to play near the top of the steep wooden staircase that led to the basement. She didn't block the stairs.

She pushed an old ottoman down them as I watched it bounce loudly down to crash into the door at the bottom. That was all the explanation I needed.

There are a few problems with feeling you must explain every time you tell your child to do something. First, you want your child to begin to obey before he has even reached the age that explanations make any sense. When you say, "No! Don't touch!" it makes no sense to tack on, "because it's hot," if your child is too young to know what "hot" is.

Another problem with feeling the need to explain is that the child will get the idea that he does not have to comply *until* you have explained. Even worse, your child may even decide you are giving him permission to disobey if he does not agree with your explanation or if he believes that you have not given an adequate or reasonable explanation. Oh, HECK, no!!!!

The child who feels entitled to an explanation is the one who asks, "Why?" when you tell him what to do. You can explain if you want to. It might be an interesting conversation, but make sure your child understands that whether you explain, or not, he *is* going to do what you tell him. Believe it or not, "Because I said so" is a perfectly viable reason. You should see the expression on the faces of some of my students when I tell them that. They clearly have never been told that before. What is *wrong* with their parents?!

My father used to tell us a little story that illustrates this. The story goes that a father and his son were in a bad car wreck. The father was badly injured and knew that he was going to lose consciousness soon. His last words to his son before passing out were, "Whatever you do, do NOT step out of this car!" What the father knew that the son did not was that they had hit a pole and dropped a power line over the car. The father knew he did not have time to explain to his son the danger of exiting the vehicle; he only had time to tell him not to. Fortunately, the father had trained his son well, and the child stayed in the car until proper assistance arrived, and his life was spared as a result.

After telling this story, my father would ask us children what the moral was. We learned to answer, "Sometimes obedience is a matter of life and death."

The worst practice I have witnessed in obedience training, though, is so prevalent that I don't know if it can ever be eradicated. This is the practice of counting to 3. You know the drill: "Marci, I'm going to count to 3, and if you haven't gotten down off that coffee table . . ." You know when Marci is going to get down, right? Not until 3. What was wrong with 1 and 2? You have just told your kid you don't really mean what you say until 3. Tell your child ONCE. Let him know you mean it the FIRST time. Whatever you were going to do to Marci when you reached 3 could just as easily be done at 1. It won't take too many times before little Marci does what you say immediately.

The same goes for the expression, "Just wait until we get home!" This only works if the first time you use it, you actually follow through. Don't you dare forget or decide to let it slide after you get home. When my mother told me, "Wait until we get home," I began to pray that I would die in a car wreck before we got there!

Better still, don't wait until you get home. Leave the grocery cart right there in the middle of the aisle if you have to and haul your brat's butt somewhere right then and take care of matters. It may mean leaving a fun time and going home immediately to impress upon your child that you will not tolerate that kind of behavior, and you do NOT drop your duties as disciplinarian just because you are in public and people might see. Let your kid know it *his* behavior that is disgraceful and not *yours*. You are not ashamed or afraid to give him what he is asking for at any time or place. It won't happen more than once or twice if you do it like I tell you.

You are the adult and the one calling the shots. Act like it.

Open House

Make your children's friends welcome in your home. Make the atmosphere of your home inviting and kid friendly so they want to be there. This way, you know where your kids are. Better yet, you know who their friends are. You can keep a closer eye on them.

Making your home kid-friendly does *not* mean that you are the permissive cool mom and all the kids want to hang at your place because you let them do whatever they want without proper supervision! I cannot stress this enough. Be vigilant in your supervision, but do things that make the kids want to stay there anyway. Bake them cookies. Let them stay for dinner. Don't get too worked up about messes, as long as they understand they have to clean them up. Don't lose your mind if they get loud. A little loudness won't kill you.

Here's another tip. Find out which kid's mom feels the same way you do about supervision and doesn't mind taking over as the host mom once in a while. I hope you can find this mom, so the two of you can share this duty and you don't get stuck with it every day.

P

Parents, Not Friends

I am sure you have heard the expression many times before that you are your child's parents, not their friends. It bears repeating, nevertheless.

Your kids will have many friends who will come and go over the years. They do not have an endless supply of parents, however. Nor are you going away.

Too many parents are afraid of making their kids angry. They refuse to tell them "No" or make them mind. They let them eat what they want, go to bed when they want, and so on. For the life of me, I cannot understand why anyone would have children if they have no intention of parenting them. If you want *friends,* then find somebody your own size!

I would never tell my friend she needs to cut back on her consumption of candy. She is an adult woman and can eat all the candy she wants. It's no one else's business, not even her BFF's. Okay, to be fair, my BFF does not have a candy problem. I know a woman, though, who literally cries because her 8 year old daughter is morbidly obese. "She just won't stop eating candy!" this woman blubbers into her tissue.

Her child is *not* her friend. This woman most certainly *can* make her little girl quit eating candy. For one thing, that kid isn't the one buying the groceries. Quit. Buying. Candy. It's not that hard. If she wants a snack, she will learn to eat fruit or crudités if that's what you provide. If she won't, she's not really hungry and is eating for the wrong reasons, anyway. Stop the bad eating habits when she is young. It may save her life. Quit worrying that she will hate you. If your kid doesn't hate you from time to time, you aren't much of a parent, anyway.

Another mother I know has a child who only eats peanut butter and chicken nuggets. Even when they are guests in someone's home, she asks the hostess to fix her kid something else to eat. She looks at the delicious spread on the table that has been prepared and declares, "Oh, he won't eat *that*." My answer is, "He will eat it when he gets hungry."

I have actually had parents argue this point with me. "Oh, you don't know *my* kid," they say. Yeah, I know your kid. I know he is going to throw an unholy wall-eyed screaming fit that may even last a while. He will sob and may even go to bed hungry. Then he'll wake up caterwauling about how hungry he is and throw himself into a sniveling heap at your feet as he pleads with you to feed him his usual. Ignore him. He'll grow tired of it and will eventually eat whatever you darn well give him to eat.

I have known kids so resistant that they will intentionally throw up the unfamiliar food when you follow through with this. Do not cave in to this manipulation. Better yet, don't let it get to this point, but if it's too late for that, then follow the advice I am giving here. He can only keep that up for so long. You are the grown-up and can outlast him.

You are not your child's friend who lets him do as he pleases. You are the parent who makes him do what is in his best interest. If he's mad, so what? He'll get over it.

Playing One Parent Against Another

This is a tactic that every child tries out at some point. Shut it down and come down hard on the kid who tries this the first time it happens.

You know how the game is played. When Mom says "No," ask Dad. When Dad says "Yes," kid skips happily away to do as he pleases while Mom and Dad fight it out. Who is in charge in this household? The kid is.

If your child asks and you give the answer they want before you know that the other parent has already denied the request, do not under any circumstances try to change the other parent's mind. You tell your kid that since they already had their answer, your answer is not, and never was, valid. Let the child know he had better not ever try that again.

If your child asks you and you know that their other parent has already given an answer, let the child know in no uncertain terms that he has a lot of nerve playing that game in your household.

Parents must be a united front, not *against* your children, but to work in your children's best interest.

Punish With a Purpose

This is a hot topic, and I could push a lot of buttons here, if I wanted to. I don't want to.

You've got parents in the "Spare the rod, spoil the child" camp and parents who have pitched their tents on the other side of the river who stick strictly to time-outs and grounding. I'm not about to tell you which one is preferable. What I *am* going to tell you is, whichever one you choose, do it right.

If you implement corporal punishment, don't do it when you are angry. Wait until you have cooled down so you don't get carried away. You are only human, and it is understandable that you are angry when your kid has done something you have explicitly told him not to do. That anger translates into extra adrenaline, though, and corporal punishment improperly administered can cause injury which you will regret when the heat of the moment has worn off. Also, make sure you apply the . . . um . . . *heat* . . . to the fleshy backside where there is not much likelihood of permanent damage. Know when to stop, too. Ignoring these rules may not only damage your child physically and emotionally, but it can also land you in jail.

If you have chosen non-physical disciplinary consequences, a good rule of thumb is to make the punishment match the crime, if at all possible. If he has not done his homework, allow him to receive a failing grade. Do not negotiate with the teacher to avoid that natural consequence and then punish him some other way. Was he careless with his electronic/cellular device and now it is broken or lost?

Too bad, so sad. Do not rush out to buy him another and believe you have punished him by giving him a stern talking to. Make him earn the money to buy the replacement. Did he forget to feed the dog again? Let him feel what it's like to be hungry by not allowing him to eat until he has fed Buster. If you really want to make an impression, don't tell him what you are doing. Eat a little snack in private so *you* won't be hungry at dinner time, and let your child *wonder* why you haven't prepared any dinner. When he starts to complain, you can drop hints until he gets it.

Punishment is one time when explaining may be in order, if your child is old enough to understand explanations. If your child does not know why you are punishing him, he may not make the connection between his behavior and the consequences. In that case, the punishment is pointless and has no effective purpose. Also, an explanation dispels the idea that your punishment is a mere retaliation against them for making you mad. Let your child know that the punishment is meant for training purposes and not retribution.

The number one rule for punishment though has already been covered – Consistency. If you don't enforce the rules every single time, your child will break them just on the chance that he might get away with it this time. They are little gamblers!

Put Yourself in Their Shoes

Every once in a while, get down on a child's level and look at situations through his eyes. This is another one of those parental balancing acts, though. Just because you see that they are angry or upset does not mean you let them have their way. Kids who are allowed to have their way all the time are monsters by the time they are 3.

All I am saying here is to be careful what you say and do. Check your words. Are they harsh and cruel, or are they spoken with a higher purpose to help your child to grow into a better person? When you must punish your child, have you made sure he understands why and that it's about him and not you? When you tell your child "No," is it because you are protecting her from something, or is it because you are being arbitrary or just don't want to be bothered with the hassle of letting her have whatever it is she is asking for?

Do you listen when your child speaks to you?

Do you attend their games and events as much as you are able, even rearranging your schedule if you have to in order to show your child he takes priority?

Does your child know without any doubt that you love her?

Many years ago, my father was closing out a sale in his tire store just before going home on a Saturday afternoon. He made the offhand comment to his customer that he was closing up shop a few minutes early so he could get home for his daughter's birthday party. The customer, scoffed and said, "Well, *my* kids know that my job comes first." He was actually proud of this fact. I have often wondered over the years what kind of relationship those children grew up to have with their father.

A job is indeed important. It provides the necessities for your family. But when the means of provision becomes more important than the people it provides for, there has been a serious mix-up in priorities.

I'm glad my Daddy understood how important it was to me that he be there for my birthday. I'm glad he *wanted* to be there. He knew that the world through my eyes saw that as more important than the last fifteen minutes of a workday.

Q

Quality versus Quantity

Some parents don't spend a lot of time with their kids. They justify this by saying something like, "Well, even if I don't have a *quantity* of time with them, at least I make sure that the time I do spend with them is *quality* time."

What a cop out.

Yes, I know we have to work and take care of responsibilities. I also know how important it is for parents to work in a little "me time," but please be careful that you are not allowing unnecessary activities to replace time with your kids. Especially, don't *avoid* spending time with your kids. Quality time is important, but who is with them when you are not? Would they be better off spending some of that time with you rather than that other person?

Consider doing some number crunching and evaluating the amount of time you spend with your kids. It is entirely possible that you will discover that the quantity of time you spend with them is adequate or that there isn't much that you can do right now to increase that time. Before deciding that, though, honestly check into it. If you can increase the amount of time you spend with your kids, I strongly urge you to do so.

Quality time does matter, but *quantities* of quality time is much better.

Quiet

ADD/ADHD is a real thing. It is also over-diagnosed. Too many little boys (and some girls, too) get into trouble at school because they cannot sit still or control their impulses. Some of them have a problem and need to be medicated. On the other hand, many of them are perfectly normal, healthy kids who just need to run off their energy. Our modern day school practices of having way too much material to cover at way too early an age is not conducive to these needs. We force kids to sit still and quiet for periods of time that their little bodies simply are not able to comply with.

Unfortunately, our society has exacerbated the problem by exposing young children to *conditioning* which makes them prone to attention deficit. Don't believe me? Spend a few minutes watching an old black and white television program. Then spend a few minutes watching a modern TV show. In the old program, the camera is set up in front of the stage set and only changes angle every so often. In the modern show, it seems the camera moves to a different view every couple of seconds. Kids spend hours in front of constantly moving video games, too. Modern children are conditioned for a constantly changing point of view. Then we set them in a desk and tell them to sit still and quiet and learn via a method that opposes that conditioning.

Many schools have adapted their methods, somewhat, but, let's face it, for a child to gain optimal access to education, sometimes he is going to have to sit down and be quiet. There is simply no other way to get the learning into his brain.

So what do we do? Letting them run and play to burn that energy off is a great idea, but they need more. They need *counter*-conditioning. They need downtime from screen-time to remove them from that constant need for ever changing entertainment so they can be *actively* taught to be *inactive*.

My mother was intuitive about these things. I could be a rambunctious little thing, and I spent a lot of time playing outside when I was little so I could get that pent up energy out of my system so I could sleep at night. But my mother took it a step further. She knew I was going to need to know how to be still and quiet when I started school.

Several mornings a week when the weather was nice, mother would take me out to the back patio. We sat in wicker patio chairs beneath the trees. She would tell me to be absolutely still and not make a peep. If I was successful, pretty soon, we'd see squirrels poking their heads out of holes in the surrounding oak trees. Mom had the unusual gift of chirruping like a squirrel. When she did this, they would cock their heads and listen. Soon they would come out of their holes and slowly make their way to the patio where we sat. It took a few mornings of trial and error to achieve this. The first time, I squealed, "A squirrel!" when I saw one peeking at us from his den. That was the end of that lesson. I progressed to keeping my mouth shut, but then I would inevitably wiggle and my chair would squeak. Back to square one. One day, though, it was my delight to have a pair of squirrels come right up to my chair. My lesson was complete the day a squirrel took a peanut from my hand.

Why was this necessary? I learned that sometimes being still and quiet is its own reward. The lessons progressed to my mother teaching me when it was okay to behave like a little hooligan and when it was not. My squirrel on the patio lessons came in real handy when we were in church or a movie theater or any place where it was more appropriate for a child to be seen and not heard.

Will this work for every child? Nope. Like I said before, conditions requiring a little pharmaceutical help are a real thing. Just don't be too quick to push drugs on your child until you know for sure. It takes a lot of time and patience to do the conditioning training my mother did. I think it was worth it.

Quit

I am talking about bad habits. Your kids will pick them up from you. If you don't want your kid to do it, then you shouldn't do it, either.

Now, I am *not* talking about grown-up activities that you get to do and kids don't. With rank comes privilege. Try to live a wholesome life practicing wholesome activities that you won't mind seeing your kids doing when they are grown up, though. You don't want to live with the regret of seeing your child grow up to do bad things and know that they are doing them because of the poor example you set.

R

Raise Them, Don't Grow Them

I recall a television movie I saw years ago starring Mac Davis. Although I don't remember much about the plot, I do remember it was about a high school football team. A parent of one of the players was kind of a no-count fellow, but he was bragging about how he had raised his boy. The character played by Davis chastised him and said something along the lines of, "You didn't raise him; he just *grew*!"

Raising kids – really *raising* them -- is hard work and long, thankless hours. Even if you don't put any effort and heart into the process, your kids will grow up anyway. If they happen to grow up to be pretty decent people despite your ineptitude, don't be too quick to take the credit for raising them.

But if they don't turn out so well, then you can take the credit for that, if you want.

Read to Them

Former First Lady Barbara Bush had the historical distinction of having been both the wife and the mother of U.S. presidents. She was also a pretty smart cookie about understanding the importance of childhood literacy and promoted it her entire life. "I'm a great believer that the most important years are the sort of early years but the preschool years and then into the first and second grades. If you get a good base in the first and second grade and you can read, you can do anything," Mrs. Bush once said. She was right.

Throughout this book, I have slipped in bits of encouragement to read to and with your children and to provide them with good reading material. I cannot stress the importance of this enough. Literacy is the foundation for learning all subjects. It opens the doors to all knowledge. If one can read, he can find any information he needs and satisfy any curiosity he has. He can escape into a foreign world or revel in one of fantasy. He will discover worlds he has not seen and may never will. He can encounter the greatest minds which ever lived, both living and dead, when he reads a book. He will meet between the covers of the book people he will never have the pleasure of meeting in the flesh. He will have access to all knowledge ever recorded, if -- and only if -- he can read.

Much has been written on the subject of the importance of reading at a young age and nurturing the habit throughout life. Data and statistics abound which support this need. I encourage you to do all you can to nurture your child's acquisition of this skill.

Please be aware that there is much more to reading than the simple decoding of the letters to recognize the words they form. Reading – real reading – is a matter of understanding that leads one to engage in critical thinking. It enhances the maturing process as you and their teachers encourage your children to consider carefully what they read and to evaluate it for merit and plausibility. This same academic skill can also be extended to provide your child with a lifelong means of recreation and pleasure, too.

It breaks my heart when I hear students say, "But I hate reading" when I encourage or require it. I heartily believe they think they hate it simply because they cannot do it well. No one truly enjoys engaging in an activity they are not good at. There is only one way to get better at it, though, and that is by knuckling down and just doing it. It's kind of a catch-22. This is why it is so vital to start them on the path to literacy at a young age. Kids love to be read to. Read to them at an early age so they associate reading with something pleasurable and not a drudgery. A good start will lead to a good race.

There is nothing in the world like reading. Make sure your child can.

Role Models Matter

You are your child's first and foremost teacher, no matter how many teachers they have while growing up. Children learn by example. Be a good one.

Kids are a classic example of "monkey see, monkey do." You may not realize it at the time, but your children are watching you. They pick up on your habits and emulate them. Even the bad habits. *Especially* the bad habits.

Do you drink, smoke, cuss, road rage? Do you have unhealthy eating habits, talk down to the waitress, live like a slob, practice bad manners? Guess what your kids are going to grow up to do and be.

Turn that around and demonstrate a better way of life for them to copy. Have some *good* habits.

S

Say "Yes"

We have already covered how to say "No" and mean it. Let's talk about "Yes" now.

Before telling your child "No," there is more to consider than just whether or not you can hold to the "No" without backing down to your child's pressure to change your mind. Ask yourself *why* you feel compelled to say "No." Is the request too expensive? Is it morally questionable? Is the timing not quite right? Is it not age appropriate? Is it dangerous? Is this one request too many, and your child has gone over his limit of requests for the month? There are plenty of reasons to deny a child's request.

On the other hand, do you feel inclined to say "No" because to say "Yes" will incur some inconvenience or unwanted expense on your part? Sometimes, that is reason enough. On the other hand, I recommend that you weigh the benefits of the request your child has made against your reluctance to grant that request. Is the trouble and expense perhaps worth it in the long run? Will your child gain some benefit such as valuable experience or a lifelong special memory from your granting the request? Is it really *that* much trouble? Although refusing to grant the request may save you some time and trouble, it might also cost your child something more.

You can have the child *earn* the "Yes," if you like. Nothing wrong with a little bartering. Then you and your child *both* get something out of the deal.

"Yes, you may go camping with your BFF's family next weekend, if you help me clean the garage *this* weekend."

"Yes, we can buy season passes to the water park, if you . . ."

Of course, you can always say "Yes" *just because*. Your kid will love that! Sometimes we, as parents, get in the habit of saying "No," because it's the easy thing to do. Sometimes a "Yes" is worth it.

Set Boundaries

Children need boundaries. They make enforcing those boundaries hard, though, because they do such a good job of challenging them! Understand that when a kid bows up against your rules, it's just what kids do. It's not so much that they don't *want* boundaries. It's more that they want to know where the boundaries *are*.

Boundaries provide security, like a fence between the safe yard and the dangerous roadway. Regardless of how much they may protest against the barriers, your child does want to feel safe. It's another need that humans have. Children are immature and do not have the ability to discern that you are acting in their best interest and not just being a big fat meanie-head. That's okay. *You* know, and that's what matters. Like all the other things they don't get, they will figure it out when they are grown.

In the meantime, hold the line. Try to keep your sanity while doing so, because this is one of the most difficult challenges of parenting you will have to face. It would be so much easier to say, "Fine! Do what you want!" and wash your hands of them when they whine or throw a tantrum. Don't. Don't even think about it. You will regret it.

And you will have failed to meet one of their primary needs.

Shaming

We hear a lot today about the subject of shaming. It's usually about body shaming such as when a female student is called out for dressing in a manner that her school has deemed inappropriate. I admit, sometimes this type of shaming is uncalled for. But let's be open-minded for a moment and make the distinction between shaming and simple dress-coding.

Shaming – true shaming -- is to imply that someone shouldn't wear a certain garment because they are too heavy, too old, too whatever. It is to say that they look unappealing in their clothing. Or, it can be an act of sexualizing an innocent child. Be careful of making that kind of call.

Dress-coding, on the other hand, is to point out that, whereas that garment may be fine at another place and time, it isn't right for school. People tend to behave the way they are dressed. Studies have been done that show it is a good idea to dress in business attire when seeking a job, even if you are doing so online or via phone. The professionalism is projected through your voice and manner.

Also, choose clothing appropriate to the venue and occasion. For example, I don't wear a swim suit to church. That's not because I am ashamed of my dimpled thighs; it's because that's not the place for that attire. Everyone has to learn this. Teach it to your children.

A child dressed in play clothes will psychologically be led to play. That's why children should have both school clothes *and* play clothes. The play clothes should not be worn to school. You don't have to send your daughter to school in a ruffled dress and Mary Janes, nor does your son have to wear a coat and tie. That's just silly. Clean jeans and a shirt that covers the shoulders and midriff (for both boys and girls) will be fine. Changing into their play clothes when they get home helps children to develop the mental distinction between school and recreation.

School dress codes are in place for a reason. Despite what media tells you, it is not always because girls are distracting to boys. Trust me. I teach for a living, and I can promise you it's usually not about that. More often than not, it is about the link between dress and behavior. You may have your doubts, but if you could spend a day in my shoes, you would see.

Having said that, though, yes, sometimes the way a child dresses *can* be distracting to other students, whether it be hormone based or just because the kid dressed to play *is* playing and diverting the other students' attention. We care about all of our students and their equal access to an education, so we do not want them distracted, whether that distraction be due to how someone is dressed or some other factor.

Also on the subject of shame is the act of instilling a sense of it in a child. Be careful how you do this. First of all, despite its bad rep, shame is not a dirty word. There are some things a person *should* be ashamed of. There is nothing quite as despicable as a person who can behave badly with impunity and yet have not one iota of shame for it.

I recall my mother occasionally saying to me, "Now, aren't you ashamed of yourself?" or "You should be ashamed!" when I had behaved egregiously. Hence, I have a developed innate sense of shame that may keep me from behaving impulsively. I think before acting and weigh the possibility that I may regret my behavior later. I assure you, that is not the only reason I behave myself, but we all have multiple constraints to our behavior; a sense of shame is just one.

Notice, my mother did *not* say, "I am ashamed of you." I hope you can see the difference!

I do not recommend overdoing it on this shaming business. Kids have tender hearts, and a little shame goes a long ways, so be judicious. Don't shy away from instilling a bit of shame when it is warranted, though.

Shielding Your Children From Reality

I have heard gruesome real life horror stories about children who have acted out behaviors they witnessed at an early age. Often, they were mimicking what they saw in a movie not intended for children. Sometimes the behavior is violent, sometimes sexual, sometimes a mix of the two. One such child was one of my students a few years back. He was 17 when he sat in my classroom. A counselor apprised me of some things he had done when he was about 5. I won't repeat them here. I can't bear to spell out such horrors. My heart is aching just remembering it now as I tell you what little I am.

His inspiration for his acts came from well-known slasher films. "Where were his parents?" you ask? They parked him in front of the TV with those DVD's in to serve as an electronic babysitter while they shot themselves up with drugs. He was a toddler at the time. Both parents OD'd and his aunt had been raising him from that point on. He bounced back and forth between her home and mental healthcare facilities.

It amazes me sometimes that we need a license to drive but not to reproduce! You can't even build a shed in your own yard in some places without a permit, but you can create a living human being and fill him with every kind of vileness imaginable.

On the opposite end of the spectrum, I had a mother take me to task once when I told her how much my children and I adored the Disney movie, *The Little Mermaid*. I couldn't imagine what she had against the film, but she enlightened me soon enough. The mermaids' breasts were covered by nothing more than coconut bras and they were thus much too scantily clad to be seen by little children. I had to admit I hadn't even noticed, which she found even more scandalous. This was the mother of *girls,* by the way, so it isn't even like she could claim she was trying to curb any boys' hormone fueled lustful thoughts.

If you are the mother who disapproves of traditional mermaid attire, I apologize. I don't mean to insult you. It's just that this is an illustration that not all parents agree on where to draw the line. If a parent is going to err, I hope that their views swing more closely to this latter example than the former, though. I'll give anti-mermaid mom that much!

So how does a parent know how much exposure is too much? Some parents judge each child individually. Clearly, if your child is prone to nightmares, you want to keep it G rated for a good while. But, even if a child does not display that he is being influenced by what he views, that doesn't mean that he isn't affected. Many children absorb and internalize, and it's hard to tell how much they are being affected.

Use some common sense. If it's scary or overtly sexual or violent, it's not for kids. Yes, they will see these things eventually, but keep it to a minimum and phase it in slowly. Most of all, hold off for as long as possible. If you discover your child has already seen something you personally would not have allowed, such as at a friend's house or via unmonitored internet access, then, by all means, turn it into a teachable moment. Discuss what he saw. Apprise him of what you do and do not approve of and why. Let him talk, too, so you can get a better idea of how much he has been affected by it.

Protect your child's heart and mind just as you protect him physically.

Know when to let go, too, though. I teach juniors and seniors in high school, and some parents can get up in arms about reading material. Obviously, what is appropriate for upper level high school would not fly in the elementary or middle school curriculum. I assure you, I have never shared with my students any prurient literature.

There is nothing wrong with being aware of what your child is reading; I encourage it, actually. But don't shield your child from good literature simply because it deals with mature themes. Even if the book does not reflect the values you impart to your child in the home, it does not mean the text is without value. Again, it may serve as an opening for a teachable moment that allows you and your child to discuss some weighty topics. You need to do that *sometime*.

Step-Parenting

I've not been a step-mom, but I have one. She's the best, by the way!

In short, love your step-children like your own. They can bring a lot of problems into a relationship, but remember they've been through a lot, whether it be their parents' divorce or a death. And now they must share a parent with someone they did not choose.

Do not resent your step-children. You knew when you married a single parent that you were getting a package deal. If you aren't willing to live with that, you shouldn't have said "I do." Does that sound harsh? Sorry, not sorry.

Often, the other biological parent can be the source of trouble. Every situation is different, so the step-parent has to deal with it the best they can. Whatever you do, you must make sure that *you* aren't the one bringing the angst. It's probably best to stay out of it and let your spouse deal with the ex.

Never ever under any circumstances badmouth the other biological parent. The child *will* take it personally, and he *will* hold it against you. There will be backlash, and it will be your fault.

To help counteract issues with other parents, make overtures of peace. Step-parents can help the children select Christmas, birthday, and Fathers/Mothers Day gifts for the "other" biological parent. By the same token, biological parents can help the children select gifts for the step-parents, as well. This is another co-parenting situation that requires maturity. Be the adult.

One of the biggest sources of trouble in the step-parenting arrangement is the issue of discipline and punishment. It may be better for the step-parent to allow the biological parent to take the lead in this area. In no way does this mean, however, that a step-parent has no authority. If a step-parent is working to contribute to the clothing, feeding, and sheltering of a child, then you better darn well believe he or she can make that kid mind! Biological parent, I'm talking to you – Do not allow your child to disrespect your spouse.

Another word of advice to step-parents – Don't put your spouse in a position where he must choose between you and their children. Blended families are hard enough already without playing those kinds of games.

No talk of "yours," "mine", and "ours." They are *all* "ours."

If everybody plays nice and fair, the kids will usually come along with time. If they don't, well they will grow up and move out eventually.

T

Take Advantage of Teachable Moments

I have addressed this in bits and pieces throughout this book so far. I hope you have understood what I mean by "teachable moments."

Not all education takes place in a classroom with textbooks or other such accoutrements. In fact, I'd venture to say that most teaching is unplanned and takes place spontaneously. When you see something of interest such as a rainbow or other natural phenomenon, point it out to your child and explain it. If you don't know the answers when they ask, then look it up together. Show them *you* are eager to learn and inspire them to hunger for knowledge, too. Instead of waiting for your kids to ask the questions (and they ask a lot of them), *you* do the asking, and show them how to find the answers. Fact finding is a valuable tool of self-sufficiency, and it's sad how many older children have no idea how to do it. This translates into an inability to problem solve, as well. These kids grow up to be handicapped adults in so many ways.

Embracing teachable moments sometimes means taking advantage of the captive moments. When my kids were small, I taught for a couple of years in a distant town, so I took them to school there so they would be near me. It was about a 45 minute commute both ways, so I had them hostage for an hour and a half five days a week. Sometimes we listened to classical music and discussed which pieces they liked or disliked and why. Often, I told them stories as I drove. At the time, they had no idea I was recounting the tales of Nathaniel Hawthorne, Washington Irving, Charles Dickens, and the like. When my daughter was a junior in high school, she was delighted to discover that she already knew the stories they were reading in her advanced placement English class, and she excelled in it. Some days, I lectured and moralized about things they didn't want to hear, but, hey, it's my car, and they couldn't get away, so . . . .

Sometimes, we just listened to Radio Disney and chilled. It is possible to kill a good thing if you overdo it!

Take Time (Because You Can't *Make* It)

I have already covered the subject of time and the issue of *quality* versus *quantities* of it. I want to interject one more reminder here, though. I know how hard it is to juggle all of the responsibilities of adulthood and still find time for our kids.

I often hear the expression that one must *make* time for the children or other important business. The truth is, no one can make time. We all have the same 24 hours in a day. A better way to describe it is to *take* time. Steal some minutes and hours away from other not so vital activities and give that time to your children when you can.

Talking to Your Kids About Sex

I hear a lot of people wonder aloud about this one. They say things like, "I'm just not sure my child is *ready*." I suspect that the person who really isn't ready for the talk is the *parent*.

I get it; I really do. This is another one of those issues that varies from child to child in how it should be handled. Some are ready at an earlier age than others, whereas some may need to wait. On top of that, the subject covers a lot of territory, and some information needs to be phased in over time. As a parent you have to decide at what age you will reveal certain things. It's a tough call. How does a parent know?

I think the key to knowing the answer is in knowing your child. You can't discuss the subject of intimacy with your children if you have a cool and distant relationship with them. You need the kind of relationship with your child that fosters ease in communication that allows for difficult conversations to evolve naturally. This requires time, and it must start early, long before the need to discuss sex has entered yours or your child's mind. Also, when you spend a lot of time with your child, it becomes easier to read his cues. It will be easier to pick up on when he is ready rather than wondering if it's time for the talk, yet.

It is especially difficult to approach the subject of sexuality with your child if the introduction to the topic is too *abrupt*. This awkwardness occurs when a parent has never had discussions with their child that serve as the precursors to the big "Talk." You begin by talking about body parts as early as toddlerhood. Name them as you wash them, if you like. Some parents insist that you have to use the proper anatomical names. Funny thing about kids, they tend to come up with their own words for stuff. I'm not sure it really matters. You can tell your son, it's a penis, but if he wants to call it Mr. Winky, that doesn't preclude you from talking about it. Heck, if calling it that makes him more comfortable to discuss it, let him. So what if he giggles? There is no law against adding a bit of levity even to serious conversations. It's akin to a spoonful of sugar helping the medicine go down.

Over time you progress to the discussion of inappropriate touching and protecting one's body, and so on. Then when the time comes for discussing intimacy, it won't be so difficult. Be direct. You can call it a "special hug" if you want to, but don't leave it at that. Kids have very good imaginations, but this is one time when their imagination won't fill in the blanks for them. You're going to have to come right out and say it.

Another important key to discussing our bodies and sexuality is to keep your tone matter-of-fact. Do not speak in ominous or serious tones. Kids hate those conversations and will avoid having them with you. That defeats the purpose. You want your child to feel comfortable enough discussing these things with you that he not only does not avoid the topic but may actually bring it up himself when the time comes. Don't be surprised if your child is the one to bring up the subject. If he does, then that is all the proof you need that it's time. Do not avoid or deflect the conversation. If he's asking, and you don't answer, he will find someone who will. This is too important to leave to an unreliable source.

Also, take care that your child does not sense that discussions about sexual matters make you uneasy. Kids pick up on that, and it gives them another reason to resist bringing you their questions and concerns.

Many parents infuse the religious aspect of teaching on sexuality as they not only must inform their children of the facts, but they also want to instill moral values such as waiting for marriage. That's great, but please take care that you do not inadvertently imply that sexuality is shameful. If you meet your child's questions with preachiness or address their natural sexual exploration with an overly punitive response, you can do a lot of damage. Although the Scriptures address that sexual behavior is to be confined to marriage, that does not mean that sex *per se* is evil. Quite the contrary; sex was *God's* idea. He created it. Be careful that you don't focus so much on the sinful aspect of sex that you fail to convey the beauty of it in its proper context. You don't want to cause any sexual hang-ups in your children that they will carry into marriage with them.

Basically, when you make it easy for your child to approach you about sexual matters, you ultimately make it easier for yourself. It becomes a natural conversation to have. Then you'll wonder why you were dreading it!

Transition With Your Children

Every parent has heard the refrain from older people that children do not stay little forever; they grow up so fast. It's true! Often, they say this with a note of sadness. As the mother of adult children, I understand this. Sometimes your heart longs for the pitter patter of little feet or an hour in a rocking chair, feeling the breath of your little one warm against your neck. There are other childhood memories you will be just as glad to see in the rearview mirror!

It doesn't all have to be a nostalgic longing for the past, though. Parenting adults can be rewarding, as well. For one thing, although you still love them as much as you ever did, you are no longer responsible for them. If you have raised them well, this will be an even greater source of relief to you.

When your children are grown, you can finally forget the earlier maxim we covered about how you are your children's parents and not their friends. You now have permission to be buddies! The relationship dynamics have completely changed.

I have discovered that my children make pretty ideal friends, in fact. Since I raised them in my value system, we share most of those values, just like I share common beliefs and standards with my other adult friends. On the other hand, your children are individuals in their own right, so they are different enough from you to keep it interesting. I love hanging out with my kids. I discuss books with my older son. I actually enjoy shopping with my daughter now, since she is the one paying for her odd fashion trends. I no longer have to reprimand my younger child for his slightly off sense of humor, since he is what he is, so I can laugh at his jokes now like I always secretly wanted to!

I feel sorry for the parents who cannot make this transition. I have seen parents ruin their relationship with their adult kids by being unable to let them go. These parents chastise their adult children for their life choices or moralize and lecture about things their kids never asked their parents' opinion about. Please try to refrain from addressing your adult children as if you are still on a higher plane. It's time for the balance you could not allow for when they were small.

Not only will attaining this balance allow you to have a rewarding relationship with your sons and daughters, but they will respect you for it, too. Don't be surprised if they come to you for advice on their own one day. If you try to force advice on them, though, they are sure to reject it. As adults, they need to establish their autonomy. If you do not allow them to do that, then you have misunderstood what your role was as a parent.

Trophies

A few years ago, the trend was started to give every child a trophy just for participating. Everyone receives the same award whether they or their team finish in first or last place. That way no one's feelings get hurt, and no child's self-esteem is damaged. I think the intentions behind the practice are good. The results, however, not so much.

Being handed a trophy may inflate the ego, but it doesn't really touch the self-esteem. It makes a pretty little dust collector on the dresser, and eventually the child matures enough that he realizes he didn't really earn it. All he did was show up. Don't try to kid a kid. He will figure out the truth about winners and losers sooner than you think. The kid who actually won doesn't feel too great about it, either.

This "everybody gets a trophy" practice in no way resembles real life. How do you feel when you have worked extra hours and put in maximum effort which has increased the company's profit margin by a substantial amount but you still get paid the same year after year as the guy who just shows up and drinks coffee at his desk until quitting time? Pretty soon, you'll be looking for a new job. At what point do we make a child aware that in the real world he will be expected to do more than just clock in?

Actually, kids learn this concept pretty well while still in school. Did you ever do group projects as a student in school? My hard working students hate those, because they know they will be the ones doing all the work. Lazy students love group projects, though. They can slip into a group with a smart kid and get the same grade just for having their name on the final product. You should see their faces when I tell them that each group member must outline exactly what he contributed to the project and present only his portion. He cannot read or present what someone else wrote or made, thinking he has fooled us into believing it is his own work. If he wants the trophy of a passing grade, he will have to do the work himself and contribute it to the group effort.

We may want to protect our children from the harsh realities of life that not everyone is a winner, but at some point they have to learn the truth. I'm afraid the abrupt revelation may be more painful than letting them learn early on that only a few can get the trophy. The kind of person produced by this misinformed practice is no prize, either.

You have to work hard to come in first place. I realize that there are a lot of people who work very hard and still never win. *They are still better off than the person who gets applauded just for putting on the uniform.* Hard work and struggling towards a goal teach all kinds of lessons which are worth far more than a wood and plastic table ornament. Point that out to your child.

Also, just because a child can't honestly earn the first place award for soccer, doesn't mean he can't place in something else. Help your child try new and different activities to find what he enjoys and can excel at. If he never wins a trophy or a ribbon, so what? You don't need to win at a thing to enjoy it. I like to bake homemade bread. There is something relaxing about kneading the dough, then punching it down after a rise. There's nothing like warm bread straight from the oven with butter slathered all over it. And that smell! I don't need to win the Pillsbury Bake-Off to enjoy that, though, do I?

A real danger caused by giving every child a trophy is that it establishes expectation in a child. He believes he will be rewarded despite his level of effort, input, or success. There isn't any incentive to try. The first time he is held accountable for producing something tangible from his efforts will come as quite a shock.

You can reward a child for participation, if you want. It's not a bad thing. A pat on the back and recognition of his effort is certainly in order. But don't take away his incentive to try harder by letting him have the winner's trophy. And don't ruin the winner's moment by making him share it with everybody else, either.

U

Unlearn Some Stuff

It is a documented fact that children tend to grow up to parent the way they were parented, themselves. Sometimes this is a bad thing.

A teacher friend of mine once told me that he remembers playing with his cousins when they were all children. His cousins always seemed to have bruises all over them, all in different stages of healing, indicating they were not the result of a single accident but of ongoing repeated injuries. This abuse was perpetrated by the parents. My friend recalls the day one of those cousins broke down crying and declared if he ever had kids, he would not treat them the way his parents treated him. Sadly, the child grew up to repeat his parents' pattern, nonetheless.

For most of us, our own parenting was a mix of successes and mistakes. Our parents are only human, and, like us, they only got one shot at it. With luck, they learned from their mess-ups and improved as we grew, and by the time we were adults, they had that parenting thing down! I know; it's kind of backwards and unfair to finally figure it all out once it doesn't really matter anymore. We survived, though, with some sweet memories and a few which make us wince a bit, but we got over those alright.

Some of you don't have too many sweet remembrances of childhood, and you have mostly memories that make you wish all they did was cause you to wince. Please take to heart my earlier admonition to put yourself in your child's shoes. It shouldn't be that hard, since you were there once, and you have some very poignant memories of what it was like. Get help. Don't let your children grow up to harbor the same bitter feelings that weigh on your heart. Ask yourself if you want your children to feel the same way about you as you do about your own parents? No? Break the pattern which started with your parents, or even with your grandparents.

Your children are precious souls which have been gifted to you. Their Creator has given you a sacred trust. Take it as seriously as it should be taken.

V

Validate Your Children

Confirm and *endorse* your child. Give him your *stamp of approval*.

I had a principal at one of the schools where I taught who came on the intercom at least once a day and told our students, "You are *valuable*; you are *complete*; you are *loved*." For many of our students, this may have been the only words of validation they had ever heard spoken over them. For some, it was a reinforcement of the validation they had already been receiving from their parents. Either way, the words were not wasted. When that principal retired, one of the things his students missed the most was hearing these words every day.

You are *valuable*; you are *complete*; you are *loved*.

Value Your Children

Parenting can be a burdensome task sometimes. Never let your children feel that *they* are a burden to you, though.

To *value* someone is to regard or esteem them highly. Your children may be little and completely untrained, but human life is a miracle. *You* have facilitated the creation of the miraculous! Be in awe. Look at your children with awe and wonder. You will never hold anything as precious as your child. Cherish and treasure them.

Someday, your job will be done, and you will release those children to the world. Will they still seem as valuable then as they were when they came to you as pure and innocent babies? Or will you have broken them and rendered them mere shells or shattered shards of the treasures they once were?

Humbling, isn't it?

Values

I think it goes without saying that one of your primary roles as a parent is to instill a moral code within your children. Teach them to discern between right and wrong and to act and make their choices accordingly. These values will govern their walk through life well beyond childhood and long after you are gone and no longer around to instruct and advise them. Neglect this duty, and you will have failed utterly as a parent and possibly unleashed a monster into the world. It sounds so dire. That's because it is.

I'm not preaching, though it may sound like it. You really don't have to be religious to see the importance of instilling values in your children. I have known avowed atheists who have taken this role of imparting moral values to their children quite seriously. For them, it was not a matter of faith or spiritualism; it came simply from their life experiences which taught them that people are much happier when they do the right thing. And they wanted their children to be happy, certainly.

Treating others well comes back to a person. Good choices avert bad consequences. A propensity to do what's right, *feels* right. No person in his right mind wants to live in chaos and surrounded by evil. Each person has a moral obligation to play his part in creating the kind of world he and everyone else wants to live in. Help your children to discover these truths early in life.

You cannot do this by lecturing or moralizing, though. No amount of preaching or proclaiming from the stump will get past a child's skin and into his heart, unless the one doing the preaching and proclaiming is living it, himself.

W

WalMart Rules

If you've ever experienced a juvenile meltdown in the middle of a department store, then you definitely know that it is something you want to avoid. I discovered early on that the best method of discipline is preventive discipline. Do everything you can to avert that disaster before it happens. It helps to see to it that your child is fed and well-rested before heading out to any public place. Let's face it; that's not always possible. Plus, when you have multiple kids, one may be rested, one may be fed, and one is who knows *what*.

I had a method that, although it wasn't always 100% fail proof, it did help immensely, so I'll share it with you. I called it the "WalMart Rules."

In our younger years when the children were small, my husband and I lived pretty close to the budget. Hence we were WalMart shoppers. A WalMart Super Center nearby also allowed for one stop shopping, which is pretty darn convenient when you're dragging three munchkins around everywhere with you. Before entering the store, I would line my kids up next to the car and ask them, "What are the WalMart Rules?" They would recite them in unison three or four times before I would take them inside.

They were as follows:

"We don't run. We don't cry. We don't ask for things."

When my daughter was 3 and 4 years old, she had quite the southern drawl, so she could stretch it out: "We don't RUUUUUUUUUUUUN. We don't CRYYYYYYYYYYYY. And we don't 'ayesk' fer thangs!"

Other women would witness this display and compliment me on my cleverness and exclaim how they wish they had thought of that when they were raising their children. My children would puff a bit with pride on being noticed for their good behavior. That always helped a bit when we got into the store, as well. Sometimes they would forget, but usually all I had to do was remind them of the WalMart rules. Occasionally, we'd have to repeat them before our shopping was done. But this practice usually helped.

Usually. Well it was better than nothing, anyway!

Whining

I pretty well covered this topic under "No" – Mean it When You Say It," since telling a kid "No" is the usual precursor to his whining. I have put this cross reference to that chapter here for you in case, in a moment of desperation, you have flipped over here, looking for some advice.

Kids whine. It's what they do, and they are good at it. It takes conditioning and retraining to put a stop to it. If you follow the advice I have given in this book, you should see your child rely less and less on this juvenile method of manipulation. I won't call it *communication*. It doesn't deserve that legitimization.

Another helpful tactic for dealing with whining is to practice selective hearing. Kids do it all the time, so we parents might as well turn the tables and use the tactic on them. Whining has a certain nasally tone that grates on the nerves. When your child approaches you with that tone, don't respond. Pretend you don't hear. He may proceed to full blown temper tantrum mode. Nip that in the bud using methods previously discussed. You may inform your child that, when he speaks in a calm and reasonable manner without that annoying whine, then, and only then, will you listen. Be consistent (always!) and eventually you might just find that your child can speak to you in a manner that does not violently pluck your last nerve like a hair band guitar player.

X

I'll bet you flipped over here first out of curiosity to see how I was going to cover this letter. Well, I cheated. You have to admit, it's kind of clever, though.

EXpectations

I have talked all throughout this book thus far about setting a high bar and equipping your child through various means to achieve those expectations. Remember, if you have low expectations, you will get minimal results. Also, remember to keep your expectations reasonable and age appropriate. You don't want your children to experience mostly failure and to become discouraged. You also want to avoid having your child feel he is a disappointment to you.

EXperiences

I read an article not too long ago that encouraged parents to give their children experiences and not just tangible gifts. I realized that my husband and I had already been doing that, and gave myself a pat on the back.

It makes sense; things break. They are also easily forgotten. I remember a few special gifts I received as a child, but most of them have long ago faded from my memory.

Experiences, on the other hand, generate lifelong memories. How many times have you heard yourself say, "Remember that time we . . . ?" Give your children the gift of those kinds of memories. It may be something relatively small such as tickets to a show they will enjoy. Or it may be big like a well-planned family vacation they have only dreamed of. Take them to new places. Take them to fun places. Take them to educational places. Take them to see where you grew up. Take them to meet people they admire.

Brainstorm and come up with some ideas and send them to me. Maybe we can add them to this book in a later edition!

EXtreme Parenting

Some parents, in an attempt to get this parenting thing right, go to extremes. They monitor every little aspect of their children's lives. They scrutinize everything from how tight the sheets are stretched when they make their beds to every expression on their kids' faces as they monitor for any signs of "attitude." They are so over the top about avoiding messes, their children won't even play with their toys, because their parents freak out over seeing their playthings anywhere but in the toy box. Often these kids are not allowed to have pets, because the parents don't want the hassle. I have noticed that these parents rarely speak to their children in a normal tone. Rather they always seem to be barking, yelling, or criticizing.

Lighten up! They're just kids, for heaven's sake! In their attempt to obtain perfection, these parents hope to produce perfect kids. Well, it's not going to happen. All they are going to get is a bunch of neurotic and unhappy people in their home.

Most parents who act like this don't see themselves objectively. In their minds, they are merely being "strict." Strict is okay, but don't get carried away.

I know one man whose teenaged son went away for a single week of summer camp. This was a farming family, so everyone, including the kids worked hard. The dad was none too happy that he had to take up the slack for his son while the boy was away. When they returned from camp, all the other kids crashed like kids do after a week of summer camp. As soon as this boy got off the bus, however, his father ordered him out to the fields to work. He yelled at him about how he had had his "fun," but he was home now and it was back to work no matter how exhausted he was. I know the dad was tired, too, but if he could cover the farm chores for a week, I don't know what harm a few more hours would have been so the poor kid could get a nap and then return to work refreshed. It was as if the father wanted to *punish* his child for having a little fun.

Let your kids be kids. Make them work, yes, but, like everything else, practice some moderation. They are only children for a little while. They have the rest of their lives to work. Instill a *work ethic* in them when they are young, but let them be kids while they still can be, too.

Y

You Get What You Get, and You Don't Throw a Fit!

I actually heard this expression the first time from one of my kids. They told me that their teacher told them this whenever a student complained or whined. I don't remember which of my children it was or which teacher, but I sure do remember this statement. It derailed many possible "episodes" in our home over the years.

Little rhyming maxims like this are catchy and easy for a child to remember. They catch on to them quickly and repeat it themselves. Sometimes all you have to do is say the first part as a reminder, and they will finish it. Disaster averted!

This phrase can shush a whiner, teach a child gratitude, and redirect an attitude.

Teacher -- whoever and wherever you are – THANK YOU!!!!!

You're the Boss

And don't you forget it. Have you ever seen a home where the children are evidently in charge? UGH!

Youth is Temporary

Hang in there. It will be over before you know it.

But remember that this means you have a lot of territory to cover in a short time. Childhood may be short, but the rest of life is long in comparison. The values and habits you instill in your children will likely follow them the rest of their lives. Do your best to get this right. You don't get any do-overs.

Z

Zip Your Lip

As a parent you will tell your children to hush or button up their lips many times over the years. It's a part of training them to know when and where it is appropriate for them to speak and what is appropriate for them to say.

There are times when you, as a parent, need to zip it up, so to speak, as well.

One of those times is when your child wants to argue with you. Never argue with a kid. It only encourages him. It takes two to argue, so if you bow out, it kind of deflates the situation. If you must say something, let it be only to repeat verbatim what you have already told him. State your demand, and when he comes back with a retort, calmly state it again. When he escalates or adds attitude, calmly state your demand verbatim again. Continue in this vain until he gets the idea that your answer is not going to change. Or you can just say nothing at all, as long as your child does not mistake your lack of response as acquiescence. After a bit, he will get the point that you meant what you said and nothing less than total and immediate obedience will be accepted.

Another time you will want to zip it up is when your child is telling you something he really needs to say. We are not talking about whining or arguing. We are talking about him confiding in you or sharing with you something from deep inside him. Listen without interrupting or judging, lest you miss something you need to hear.

Zits and Hormones

The teenage years can be a challenge, but try to enjoy them, nevertheless. This is still your child you are dealing with, although it may seem he has gone underground for a while, hidden by angst and attitude. Hang in there. He will re-emerge on the other side just fine, if you don't give up on him and just love him through it. You were a teenager once, yourself. You made it through. So did your parents. You got this!

Zucchini Principal

Before I go, I would like to close out this little book with a bit of general good advice I call the Zucchini Principle. It's a good principle to cover a lot of problem areas in life, child-rearing included.

I do not garden. I had a rock garden once, but it wilted. I know a few people with green thumbs, though, and they are fond of keeping me supplied with an endless cache of zucchini squash. Whereas many garden plants need regular attention and specific conditions in order to produce, humble zucchini seems to proliferate in any weather and soil conditions and with any level of care or lack thereof. My friends come by every week, sometimes more often, with bags filled with their surplus zucchini. They come beaming as if they are doing me a favor, but there is a tacit understanding that I am the generous one as I relieve them of their vegetable burden.

I bake it, fry it, sauté it, and grind it up and hide it in casseroles. Put through a food processor, zucchini makes a delicious bread with the flavor and texture of pumpkin when mixed with the right spices. Eventually, though, I inevitably end up with more zucchini than I have recipes and certainly more than my family wants to eat. Although I am always grateful for the gifts of garden bounty, there will always be too much zucchini.

In its insistence on defying limitation, zucchini is a symbolic reminder to me of the need for moderation in all things. Too much of a good thing is never good, whether it be food, alcohol, sugar, salt, or any other thing a person might delight in. This includes zucchini.

Moderation matters in bringing up children, too. You want your child to have fun, but you know you must teach him that life is not all fun and games. You can't swing to the other extreme and turn your child into a work horse, either, though. Discipline is a good thing, but every once in a while, everybody needs to let his hair down. From time to time, it will be necessary to punish your child. If the only interaction you have with your child is to administer punishment, though, neither you nor your child is benefitting. Also, if repeated punishment is not yielding the desired results, you are clearly doing it wrong, or are not using an effective method. Sometimes, for your child's well-being, you must tell him "No." On the other hand, there are many times that a child can get a lot of good out of a well-timed "Yes."

The point is, don't overwhelm your child with too much of any one thing. Moderate. A person can only handle so much zucchini.

About the Expert

Melanie Miller is a high school English teacher and the mother of 3 adult children. She has long said that she has had enough experiences with children and enough stories to fill a book, so that is exactly what she has done! She has learned a lot about kids over the years and has some great stories and helpful advice to share.

Her greatest achievement, Melanie claims, is that she has managed to raise 3 human beings to successful and self-supporting adulthood without losing her mind in the process or causing any permanent damage to her kids. If you would like to hear how she did that, then this book is for you.

Melanie's other interests are reading, free lance writing, trying out new restaurants, and lounging around with her three dogs and cat with which she has filled her nest so it doesn't feel quite so empty.

HowExpert publishes quick 'how to' guides on all topics from A to Z by everyday experts. Visit HowExpert.com to learn more.

Recommended Resources

- HowExpert.com – Quick 'How To' Guides on All Topics by Everyday Experts.
- HowExpert.com/books – HowExpert Books
- HowExpert.com/products – HowExpert Products
- HowExpert.com/courses – HowExpert Courses
- HowExpert.com/clothing – HowExpert Clothing
- HowExpert.com/membership – Learn All Topics from A to Z by Real Experts.
- HowExpert.com/affiliates – HowExpert Affiliate Program
- HowExpert.com/jobs – HowExpert Jobs
- HowExpert.com/writers – Write About Your #1 Passion/Knowledge/Expertise.
- YouTube.com/HowExpert – Subscribe to HowExpert YouTube.
- Instagram.com/HowExpert – Follow HowExpert on Instagram.
- Facebook.com/HowExpert – Follow HowExpert on Facebook.

CPSIA information can be obtained
at www.ICGtesting.com
Printed in the USA
LVHW082020231219
641450LV00011B/246/P